THE HISTORY OF
CANMORE

Rob Alexander

Summerthought

Banff, Alberta

THE HISTORY OF CANMORE

Published by

Summerthought

Summerthought Publishing
PO Box 2309
Banff, AB T1L 1C1
Canada
www.summerthought.com

1st edition —2010

Text copyright © 2010 by Rob Alexander

All rights reserved. No part of this book may be translated, transmitted or reproduced in any form, except brief extracts for the purpose of a review, without prior written permission of the publisher or a licence from the Canadian Copyright Licensing Agency (Access Copyright). For a copyright licence, visit www.accesscopyright.ca or call (800) 893-5777.

Printed in Canada by Friesens

We gratefully acknowledge the financial support of the Alberta Foundation for the Arts for our publishing activities.

Library and Archives Canada Cataloguing in Publication

Alexander, Rob, 1969-
The history of Canmore / Rob Alexander.

Includes bibliographical references and index.
ISBN 978-0-9811491-5-8

1. Canmore (Alta.)—History. I. Title.

FC3699.C35A53 2010   971.23'32   C2009-907130-4

Table of Contents

Introduction 1

Chapter 1 Origins 7

Chapter 2 Exploration 23

Chapter 3 Railway 41

Chapter 4 Growth 53

Chapter 5 Prospecting 61

Chapter 6 Mining 69

Chapter 7 A New Century 95

Chapter 8 The End of an Era 133

Chapter 9 Recent Times 147

Timeline 172

Further Reading 174

Index 176

Photo Credits 186

Acknowledgments 187

About the Author 188

Introduction

Situated alongside the sparkling blue waters of the Bow River, with the distinctive Three Sisters as a backdrop, the town of Canmore is today known around the world for its natural beauty and endless opportunities for outdoor activities such as hiking, climbing, biking, and golfing. An interesting downtown core dotted with stylish boutiques and upscale restaurants adds to the charm.

While experiencing the wonders of modern Canmore, it is difficult to comprehend how far the town has come since the Canadian Pacific Railway (CPR) first laid a rail line through the Bow Valley in 1883. Before European settlement occurred, which followed the arrival of the railway, the valley was home to nomadic human visitors for over 10,000 years. These ancient people left their impressions of the Bow Valley in the form of rock art. This art depicts the earliest-known history of humans in the Canmore area.

In 1871, just four years after confederation, the colony of British Columbia agreed to join the eastern provinces as part of Canada if the Canadian government built a railway linking the west coast to the rest of the country. Construction eventually began in 1880, and the end of the rail line reached the frontier city of Calgary in 1883. A few months later, the line reached the site of what is now Canmore. Originally known as Siding 27, it was a small depot built to store and service locomotives and house crews crossing the Continental Divide at Kicking Horse Pass.

Although he had never seen the mountainous western portion of the continent, Prime Minister John A. Macdonald's dream was realized on November 7, 1885, when the last spike was driven into the rail line at Craigellachie. By this time, Siding 27 had been renamed Canmore and prospectors had spread throughout the Bow Valley. Settlement quickly expanded from the rail line south to the Bow River, where coal mining had begun in earnest by the end of the 1880s. By this time, the town was thriving. The mining operations attracted workers from around the world, while the town itself boasted a busy main street lined with businesses, an

Introduction

Canmore Opera House

opera house, and lots of sporting teams. Mining was at the forefront of the local economy until 1979, when the last coal mine closed. Since that time, tourism and resort development have become Canmore's primary industries.

Today, Canmore enjoys a unique sense of place. It is a town that has evolved immensely over the last two decades—yet fragments of the past are inextricably intertwined with modern life.

While historic photographs of the town and its people do an admirable job of providing a record of the past, Canmore is fortunate to have a cross-section of buildings that provide a more direct link to the past. Although many of Canmore's oldest structures have been demolished to make room for new construction, thankfully, resident volunteers began working to save Canmore's history in the 1980s. Groups such as the Canmore Centennial Museum Society, landowners who have worked with all levels of government to save Canmore's heritage buildings, and individuals such as the late Norman Witham, who donated his collection of maps and photographs to the museum, have all contributed to the preservation of the town's history.

A casual observer may not notice many things about Canmore today that make an overt connection to the town's railway and coal mining history. But like the exposed seams of coal that attracted the first prospectors, hints of history are dotted throughout town and its surroundings—one just needs to look carefully. The Canmore Museum & Geoscience Centre is a solid foundation for the preservation and enjoyment of the town's history. Those with a link to Canmore's past entrust the museum with their artifacts and stories—both of which are exceedingly important to ensure we understand the full story of Canmore. One can view a handful of original miners' cottages and the privately owned McNeill House, stroll through the North West Mounted Police (NWMP) Barracks, enjoy a drink at the Canmore Hotel, take in a show at the Canmore Miners' Union Hall, wander through reclaimed mine sites, or admire the attention to detail in the Ralph Connor Memorial United and St. Michael's Anglican churches.

The History of Canmore is the fourth volume to chronicle the town's history. Like previous books dating back to Edna Appleby's

Links to Canmore's mining history are dotted through the valley, including this concrete shell, which was a lamphouse at the entrance to No. 2 Mine.

Introduction

Canmore's Three Sisters remain a local landmark, well over a century since this photo was taken in the 1880s.

Canmore: The Story of an Era (1975), this book is designed to entertain readers and educate them on lesser-known stories of the past through extensive research and newly discovered images—including the first published portrait of coal mine operator Hobart W. McNeill. *The History of Canmore* is limited only by the fact that numerous details pertaining to Canmore's history have yet to be teased from the historical fabric scattered among institutions and private collections throughout Canada and beyond.

1 Origins

The History of Canmore

Although the story of Canmore begins in 1883, with the arrival of the Canadian Pacific Railway, the history of humans in the Bow Valley dates back thousands of years. It is common to assume that the valley was a primitive, dangerous landscape that blocked travel and inspired fear, but this is far from the truth.

Eleven thousand years ago, during the last ice age, the Canadian Rockies were a harsh, unforgiving, and frigid landscape with a massive sheet of ice extending across most of the mountain range. At this time, the air temperature was an estimated four degrees lower than it is today. Also, the amount of annual precipitation was double the amount that falls today. As a warming trend began and the ice began receding northward, ice age megafauna such as mammoths, giant bison, and huge bighorn sheep, as well as caribou, elk, deer, wolves, and bears migrated into the valley from the plains. These animals were closely followed by Paleo-Indian hunters.

Archaeologists have found evidence suggesting the first human visitors to the Bow Valley were highly mobile and moved with ease across mountain passes to trade, hunt big game, and quarry rock for tools and weapons. Over 35 prehistoric sites have been identified in the Bow Valley. The oldest of these sites are 30 kilometres west of Canmore along the shore of Lake Minnewanka in Banff National Park, and 50 kilometres east of town at Sibbald Flats in Kananaskis Country. At these sites, researchers have excavated 11,000-year-old stone tools and projectile points. Evidence of hunter-gatherers living along the north shore of Vermilion Lakes, in Banff National Park, dates back an estimated 10,700 years. On the benchlands overlooking the Trans-Canada Highway between Canmore and Banff, researchers discovered a small cooking hearth that dates back approximately 9,600. With the exception of Old Crow and Bluefish caves in the Yukon, which date back 15,000 years, these Bow Valley sites are older than most archaeological sites in Canada.

The oldest evidence of human habitation within what are now the Canmore town limits is found in the form of two 7,700-year-

Origins

> ## Prehistoric Life
>
> Around 750 million years ago, a warm, shallow sea fringed by swamp-rich jungles covered what is now Alberta. Today, the Bow Valley is around 600 kilometres from the closest ocean and much further from the tropics. However, signs of both ocean life and jungle plants are evident locally in the fossilized remains of ferns, trees, shells, coral, reef-building sponges, trilobites, snails, and even fish. When tectonic forces began forming the Rocky Mountains, around 70 million years ago, sediment on the ocean floor was thrust upwards, which means that today you may even find coral on local mountain tops.
>
> One of the most interesting fossils found in the Bow Valley was the jawbone from a 10-metre long fish estimated to have lived about 350 million years ago. Bony plates covered this nearly four-ton carnivorous fish providing it with thick armour that covered its body and gave it savage-looking, beak-like jawbones. While *Dunkleosteus* plates are extremely rare, many other fossils are commonly found in the Bow Valley. Corals and shells are the most abundant, with other interesting fragments appearing now and then to the patient and relatively trained eye.
>
> The Canmore Museum & Geoscience Centre has an interesting exhibit of locally collected fossils, including a 540-kilogram petrified Cyprus tree trunk. The trunk was found in a coal seam at what is now Three Sisters Mountain Village, with its tree rings and bark still visible.

old sites along the Bow River, near the Canmore Golf and Curling Club. Prehistoric sites have also been unearthed on the benchlands along the northern edge of town. Camps and bison kill sites of a similar vintage have also been discovered beyond the town limits near the base of Mount Yamnuska, Harvie Heights, Exshaw, Lac des Arcs, Heart Creek, and in Bow Valley Provincial Park. East of Canmore, where the mountains give way to foothills, evidence shows how hunters used cliffs as buffalo jumping pounds. They would drive the bison off the cliffs and onto the river ice below.

The potential for discovery of even older sites is possible. In a silt-filled bedrock basin beside Lac des Arcs, archaeologists excavated bone fragments, fire-broken rocks, and a single projectile point belonging to people classified as the Pelican Lake Phase. The researchers also identified an ancient soil known as *paleosol*, which was found at the lowest level of the Vermilion Lakes sites. Within this 11,000-year-old dirt is the promise of more remarkable archaeological finds that will serve to provide an even clearer picture of the early inhabitants of the Bow Valley.

But who exactly were the first inhabitants of the Bow Valley? The question of how the earliest nomadic hunter-gatherers reached the Bow Valley remains open, although two theories are

Bison in the Bow Valley

In 2004, workers at a construction site in downtown Banff discovered two intact bison skulls buried under a thick layer of silt and gravel. The animals were likely swept down the Bow River during a flood and slowly buried beneath layers of gravel and mud. To date, the oldest bison remains discovered in the valley are at least 9,000 years old and were found in a prehistoric campground along the shore of Lake Minnewanka. Further east, a 7,000-year-old bison kill site was found near Heart Creek, while the left hind leg of a bison killed by prehistoric hunters was found along the shore of Lac des Arcs, four metres below the surface.

Although bison, also known as buffalo, were a part of the Bow Valley ecosystem for a considerable length of time, they may have only lived in the valley during the given credence by archaeologists. The first suggests they followed an ice-free corridor between the Cordilleran and Laurentide ice sheets that covered much of Canada at the time. The other theory suggests that the first North Americans used crude boats to follow the Pacific coastline. It is possible that early people used both routes to travel from the Beringia land bridge, which linked Alaska and Asia during the Ice Age, south onto the plains before spreading out and, over generations, moving northward as the ice age ended.

winter to escape the harsh weather conditions found on the prairies, according to research conducted by Cliff White, a former Banff National Park biologist, and Charles Kay, an American wildlife ecologist. According to the research of these two experts, at one time bison were the second most common ungulate in the Canadian Rockies (only bighorn sheep were present in greater numbers). White and Kay found that between 1792 and 1872, the members of 26 different expeditions to the region recorded 19 signs of bison and 39 sightings. The members of these expeditions also recorded killing a total of 34 of these animals. In the early 1800s, explorer and mapmaker David Thompson recorded his encounter with a small herd of bison near Howse Pass in Banff National Park. Alexander Henry, an early trader and explorer, reported in 1811 that he found signs of bison on the Kootenay Plains. North America's bison population peaked at approximately 30 to 70 million, but by 1890, the herds had been decimated, leaving the bison nearly extinct in the wild, including the Bow Valley.

Bison returned to the Bow Valley in 1897 when three calves arrived in Banff from Texas, followed by the arrival of 13 plains bison from Manitoba. The Manitoba bison were a gift to the government of Canada from Sir Donald Smith, a director of the Canadian Pacific Railway. One of these animals was a 26-year-old bull affectionately referred to as "Sir Donald." This bison was one of the last born in the wild and the largest bull on record at that time. The fenced herd grew in 1911, when 77 plains bison, including 7 bulls, were brought to Banff from Montana by Norman Luxton and Howard Douglas, the superintendent of Rocky Mountains Park (now Banff National Park).

Banff's bison paddock was torn down and the bison were moved to Elk Island National Park following approval of the 1997 Banff National Park Management Plan, which sought to clear a path to allow wildlife an unimpeded corridor around the town of Banff. Today, in an effort to restore an important and long-absent part of the landscape, Parks Canada, with support from the Eleanor Luxton Historical Foundation is looking at the feasibility of reintroducing plains bison into Banff National Park.

The Clovis, prehistoric Paleoindian hunters first identified at a bison kill site in Clovis, New Mexico, in the mid-1930s were for many years believed to have been the first inhabitants of North America, colonizing it from via the Beringia land bridge some 12,000 years ago. New research is proving the Clovis were not the first human beings to reach North America. However, the types of tools and points found at Lake Minnewanka and Sibbald Flats suggest that they were the first people to inhabit the Bow Valley. The Clovis, who are known for their distinctive fluted spear points, were highly successful big game hunters. As they spread through the continent's western regions, the Clovis hunted bison, bighorn sheep, caribou, and mammoths.

Archaeologists have yet to discover Clovis sites within the immediate vicinity of Canmore that rival the age of the Bow Valley's earliest sites. However, if these early ice age hunters did indeed camp and hunt along the shores of Lake Minnewanka and Vermilion Lakes, on the benchlands near Banff, and at Sibbald Flats, it is reasonable to believe that the same hunters camped along the Bow River where the town of Canmore lies today.

About 10,500 years ago, it appears the Clovis were replaced by a culture known as the Folsom. It is unknown whether or not the Folsom were actually the Clovis with a more evolved culture and improved hunting tools. What is known, however, is that each subsequent culture developed increasingly sophisticated technological groups, which are referred to as phases, periods or traditions, that replaced one another throughout North America's early history all the way to the time of the arrival of the Europeans.

As archaeologists find new sites, they broaden society's understanding of the Bow Valley's first human inhabitants. Recent discoveries have given researchers a better idea of how well the Plains-dwelling Besant people adapted to life in the mountains around 7,000 years ago. Archaeologists recently excavated a site in Banff National Park, in 2008, and another east of Exshaw on the Stoney Nakoda Reserve, in 2009. Parks Canada archaeologists Gwyn Langemann and Bill Perry discovered that the Banff

An archeological dig site in the Bow Valley.

National Park site, located on the banks of the Bow River near the junction of the Trans-Canada Highway and the Bow Valley Parkway, had been used continuously for at least 7,000 years. The 30,000-square-metre site, of which only a fraction was investigated during two summers of fieldwork, offered up a trove of arrowheads, scrapers, and small stone blades.

To the east, near Hector Lake located on the Stoney-Nakoda reserve, archaeologists working for the provincial government as part of a project to realign and widen the Highway 1A, found a similar story of continuous use over thousands of years at a site also linked to the Besant. Here, Sean Goldsmith and Dan Wyman of Bison Historical Services, a Calgary company that specializes in cultural resource management, found a large quantity of fire-broken rock, indicating that people had dropped fire-heated rocks into hide-lined pits to boil water and render fat. They also found small hide scrapers, arrowheads, and numerous rock flakes knapped from Montana and Banff chert, as well as obsidian

> ## Columbia Plateau Tradition
>
> The Columbia Plateau Tradition is a modern term used to describe loosely connected groups of Aboriginal people, including the Interior Salish (Shuswap, Flathead and Pend d'Oreille) and the Kootenay (also spelled Kutenai and Kootenai), who lived west of the Continental Divide and shared a similar culture and technology.

brought to the region from Idaho or Wyoming through early trade networks. Both these sites, along with others unearthed throughout the Canadian Rockies, demonstrate that even though the mountains provide a difficult environment for human habitation, they can also be a place where people can thrive. Overall, it appears the Besant had been regular visitors to the Bow Valley until 850 years ago.

The Kootenay, although part of Columbia Plateau Tradition west of the Continental Divide, have a long history in the Bow Valley. Their roots extend throughout the Rocky Mountains, along the Foothills, and onto the Great Plains. They could be described as the true mountain people. The Kootenay, whose language has no connections to any other Aboriginal group in Canada, believe their ancestors emerged from a hole located east of the Rocky Mountains. The ancient Kootenay, who moved with the seasons between the eastern slopes of the Canadian Rockies, including the Bow Valley and the Columbia Valley, were pushed west over the mountains into the Columbia Valley by disease and pressure from the aggressive and more numerous members of the Blackfoot Confederacy.

Eventually, the descendants of these early bands of Kootenay separated into two branches. The Lower Kootenay became a water culture, relying on fish and waterfowl, while the Upper Kootenay maintained their Plains lifestyle, which often included annual forays over the Continental Divide and onto the prairies to hunt bison. They followed this path until the 1880s, when the bison became extinct in what is now Alberta due to over-hunting.

Like the Kootenay, the Shuswap, also known as the Kinbasket First Nation, located in the Columbia Valley are an Aboriginal group from west of the Continental Divide with a connection to the Bow Valley. Historical evidence of the Shuswap can be found at the Banff Springs Golf Course. On the Bow Flats near the confluence of the Spray and Bow Rivers, round depressions indicate the presence of eight pit houses used by the Shuswap. These pit houses date back 2,800 years and appear to have been last used roughly 400 years ago.

As the Kootenay and Shuswap left the Plains, Foothills and eastern Rockies, the Blackfoot (Siksika), who were allied with the Peigan (Piikani), Blood (Kainai) and T'suu Tina, filled the void. While these four groups were primarily Plains dwellers, they were drawn into the mountains to hunt. They also journeyed to the mountains for spiritual reasons.

Even though the nations of the Blackfoot Confederacy ventured into the mountains, it was the Stoney, or Nakoda, as they prefer to refer to themselves, which means "The People," who would eventually replace the Kootenay as the people of the Bow

This dart point was excavated from an ancient campsite near Morley.

Valley. The Blackfoot and Blood referred to the Stoney as the mountain dwellers, according to Ian Getty and Erik D. Gooding in the *Handbook of North American Indians*. A part of the Great Sioux Nation, the Stoney, named for their practice of cooking with hot stones, and their Assiniboine relatives, are descendants of the Dakota Sioux who fled the upper Missouri River region in the early-1600s during a smallpox epidemic. The Stoney reached the Foothills in what is now Alberta in two main groups during the mid-1600s. Travelling westward, one group reached the Rocky Mountains south of the international border then turned north, while the other group headed west through what is now Alberta. Together, the bands settled in an area that stretched from the Brazeau River in the north down beyond Chief Mountain, south of the Alberta-Montana border. Once settled along the eastern slopes of the Canadian Rockies, the Stoney developed a distinct mountain culture while still maintaining some of their core traditional Plains ways of life. The three bands that comprise the Stoney Nakoda First Nation, Bearspaw, Chiniki, and Wesley, also developed distinct characteristics.

The Chiniki, who came to call the Bow, Spray, and Kananaskis valleys home, hunted bighorn sheep and deer, as well as bison. The more southern Bearspaw band continued to hunt bison on the Plains, while the Wesley focused on elk, moose, and deer. The Stoney were also known to cross the Continental Divide to trade with the Shuswap and Kootenay. Closer to Edmonton, the ancestors of the Alexis and Paul bands were once known as the Wood Stoney, as their lifestyle focused more on hunting, trapping, and fishing in the forests and Foothills.

Peter Erasmus, who served as a guide and interpreter for explorer James Hector in the late 1850s, described the Stoney as a peaceful people with a policy of avoiding trouble, unlike their Plains neighbours, the Blackfoot. He wrote that the Stoney raised sturdy and sought-after horses. He also noted that they were recognized for their tracking skills and that no other tribe could match their use of medicine.

Walking Buffalo in 1938.

Walking Buffalo

Lots of people hardly even feel real soil under their feet, see plants grow except in flower pots, or get far enough beyond the street lights to catch the enchantment of a night sky studded with stars. When people live far from scenes of the Great Spirit's making, it's easy for them to forget his laws.

—Walking Buffalo

Tatanga Mani, or "Walking Buffalo," born in 1871 east of Canmore along the Bow River, was a chief, medicine man, and highly respected elder of the Stoney Nakoda First Nation.

As a child, Walking Buffalo was adopted by Methodist missionary John McLean, who named him George McLean after his mother passed away. Through his teenage years, Walking Buffalo witnessed the end of traditional life for the Aboriginal people of the West, including the disappearance of the bison. Even though the world of his parents and grandparents changed dramatically in his lifetime, he advocated peace, harmony, and acceptance of all people, Aboriginal and non-Aboriginal alike, and a love and deep respect for the natural world.

In 1958, at the age of 87, Walking Buffalo, along with a small group of Aboriginal people, toured twenty-seven countries over four months. He shared his message with everyone who would listen; he advocated that it was not right to raise children away from nature. Throughout his tour of the world, Walking Buffalo urged people to accept the Aboriginal people and to be open to their beliefs and history. He also sought to ensure Canada's Aboriginal people maintained their rich culture. As part of that deep-seated goal, Walking Buffalo helped found the Buffalo Nations Cultural Society, which has operated Banff's Buffalo Nations Luxton Museum.

Walking Buffalo passed away on December 26, 1967, at the age of 96.

In summer, the Stoney lived in portable bison-hide tipis. They moved into more permanent tipi-shaped lodges covered with spruce bark, moss, and mud in the winter. Evidence that the Stoney lived and were comfortable in the Bow Valley can be found in the landscape. Before Europeans arrived and began giving the mountains the names that we use today, the Stoney had already named the prominent features in this region. In Stoney, Canmore is referred to as *Chuwapchi_pchi_yan Kude Bi*, or the place where a hunter was fooled into thinking a stump was something else, either an animal or an enemy, depending on the story. One of these tell the story of a young hunter who shot at what he thought was an animal lurking in a group of willows but instead turned out to be a stump. The other tells of a jumpy Stoney warrior who shot at a small tree in the darkness thinking it was a Blackfoot warrior. According to this story, Stoney warriors killed a Blackfoot warrior earlier in the day during a battle further west, so it is understandable that his mind would play tricks on him as he peered into the darkness.

The Bow River was known to the Stoney as *I jathibe Wapta*. Hunters and warriors would use Saskatoon saplings growing along the river banks to make their bows. Currently, the Stoney tend to refer to the Bow River as *Mi ni thni Wapta*, which means "Cold Water River," an accurate description even in summer.

East of Canmore, facing the hamlet of Dead Man's Flats, is Wind Ridge. This long ridge rises over Wind Valley, but is dwarfed by Mount Lougheed and Windtower. The valley and its guardian peaks could easily be called one of the most beautiful spots in the Bow Valley. The Stoney were familiar with this valley and its ridge. They called the ridge *Ganutha I_mpa*, which means "Windy Point." Closer to Canmore, the aspen and poplar-filled meadow that sits at the edge of Elk Run Boulevard, known locally as Indian Flats, was called *Tinda Meemum*, or "Round Clearing." It was here the Stoney camped when they travelled between Morley and Banff.

Carved by wind, rain, and glaciation, the three iconic hoodoos on the northern benchland overlooking Canmore and the Bow

Origins

Valley were believed to have been created by *Inktomni*, "The Trickster." This mythological giant, who is credited by the Stoney with creating the land and its inhabitants, shaped the hoodoos out of dirt, then told the Stoney that they were their tipis. His trick led them to begin making their own tipis.

Bow Valley Pictographs

One of the most important resources for learning about the valley's earliest inhabitants are pictographs (rock art), which appear at Grassi Lakes, Grotto Canyon, and Rat's Nest Cave. Dating between 1,000 and 1,500 years old, these intriguing paintings created with red ochre tell remarkable stories of how early Paleo-Indians perceived the Bow Valley and provide a record of their spiritual beliefs.

People belonging to the Columbia Plateau Tradition, a cultural affiliation that stretches from the western edge of Alberta into central British Columbia and parts of Washington, Oregon, Idaho and Montana, travelled to secluded spots in the mountains to fast, pray, and seek guidance from the spirits. Evidence of these spiritual journeys, or vision quests, can be found in the pictographs painted in deep-red ochre on a large boulder sitting in the middle of the narrow canyon above Grassi Lakes. These pictographs may have been painted by the ancestors of the Kootenay (Ktunaxa) or Interior Salish. They include a hunting scene of what appears to be a figure throwing a spear at a caribou, a small series of vertical lines known as tally marks and a human figure—recognized as Alberta's best-preserved pictograph—holding what appears to be a hoop or drum. A series of ochre handprints can be found nearby as well.

Tally marks may indicate the number of days spent at the site or the number of rituals performed. The hunting scene may represent thanks offered to the spirits and the animals for a successful hunt or favour sought for an upcoming hunt. The scene may also have been painted to control animal spirits or to help teach younger hunters.

According to James D. Keyser and Michael A. Klassen in their book *Plains Indian Rock Art*, the pictographs of Grassi Lakes may be connected to the ancestors of today's Kootenay and Shuswap. Stoney Nakoda historian Ian Getty, however, points out that the connection of these western groups to the Columbia Plateau Tradition is only one possibility, as no one can say with certainty who created the pictographs.

Pictographs are a delicate resource. Please do not touch or pour water on this ancient art, as both will damage them.

Treaty 7

Treaty 7 was a peace treaty between the Government of Canada and the Tsuu T'ina (Sarcee), the Stoney (Bearspaw, Chiniki, and Wesley/Goodstoney) and the Blackfoot Confederacy, which was comprised of the Siksika (Blackfoot), Piikani (Peigan) and Kainaiwa (Blood).

It was signed on September 22, 1877, at Blackfoot Crossing, a picturesque location east of Calgary along the Bow River where a gravel bar offered an easy ford across the river.

The treaty stated: "the Blackfeet, Blood, Peigan, Sarcee, Stoney and other Indians inhabiting the district hereinafter more fully described and defined, do hereby cede, release, surrender, and yield up to the Government of Canada for her Majesty the Queen and her successors for ever, all their rights, titles, and privileges whatsoever to the lands included within the following limits …"

In return, the government offered to provide land set aside as reserves for each nation, as well as education, farm equipment, and treaty payments. Due to misunderstandings arising from poor translation and the fact that the Aboriginal people had no concept of or terms for land title, it is likely they did not understand the agreement they had made.

The Aboriginal nations believed they were signing a peace treaty that would allow Europeans to live among them on the vast lands of what was then the North-West Territories (including most of what is now Alberta). The Dominion of Canada and the British Crown, however, acknowledged the signing as total surrender. The government believed that negotiating and securing the surrender of the Blackfoot Confederacy was the only option available for opening the West to settlement and development. The Royal Proclamation of 1763 stated that settlement could not occur on land occupied by Aboriginal people. With their traditional ways of life coming to an end as the bison disappeared, the seven nations felt they had no choice.

All three bands of the Stoney Nakoda First Nation were placed on a 109-square-mile reserve that flanked the Bow River in the traditional territory of the Chiniki band, located just east of Canmore. The Wesley and Bearspaw bands later petitioned the government for separate reserves at Bighorn and Eden Valley, and these were established in 1948.

Today, the Treaty 7 Management Corporation (www.treaty7.org) works to administer services and improve opportunities for the Treaty 7 nations. Blackfoot Crossing is now home to an impressive interpretive centre.

Stoney names demonstrate an intimacy with the Bow Valley, and the stories connected to the names express a respect for the beauty and majesty of the Rocky Mountains.

The growing influence of the fur trade, which began in the early 1600s but did not reach the West until the mid-1750s, meant their world was shrinking. Due to a lack of beavers, fur traders had shown no interest in the Bow Valley until competition between the Hudson's Bay Company and the North West Company forced the two competitors to expand beyond the traditional fur trade routes of central and northern Canada. The first fur trade post in Alberta was built by Peter Pond in 1778 next to the Athabasca River, which begins in Jasper National Park and flows north past Edmonton. Fort Edmonton was built in 1795. The Stoney traded at both posts, but Rocky Mountain House, established in 1799 and located closer to the Bow Valley, became their main centre for trade.

Even though the Stoney were influenced by the fur trade and the introduction of European goods, specifically the horse and the gun, they did not see Europeans in the Bow Valley until 1800, when David Thompson and a small group of fur traders arrived.

Today, the three bands of the Stoney Nakoda First Nation share a reserve at Morley, which was established as part of the Treaty 7 agreement. The reserve is on a portion of the traditional land of the Chiniki band, along the Bow River east of Canmore. The Wesley and Bearspaw bands also have smaller reserves, where band members continue to live on their traditional lands. The modern Stoney Nakoda Resort is located on the Morley reserve along the Trans-Canada Highway. The reserve is also home to a restaurant specializing in native cuisine, a large arena, a trades' school, and schools for Grades 1-12, where an ever-increasing number of students graduate annually.

2 Exploration

On a cold day in late November 1800, fur trader, explorer, and surveyor David Thompson stood on the slopes of Loder Peak and looked out over the Bow Valley. In his journal, Thompson described the view to the east as "vast and unbounded," and in the west the "hills and rocks rose to our view covered with snow, here rising, there subsiding, their tops nearly of an equal height everywhere. Never before did I observe so close a resemblance to the waves of the ocean during a wintry storm. In viewing their wild appearance the imagination is apt to say that these mountains must once have been liquid, and when in that state, swelled

> ## The Journals of David Thompson
>
> David Thompson, the first non-Aboriginal person to visit the Bow Valley, eloquently described his November 1800 visit as such:
>
> *Our View from the Heights to the Eastward was vast & unbounded – the Eye had not Strength to discriminate its Termination: to the Westward Hills & Rocks rose to our View covered with Snow, here rising, there subsiding, but their Tops nearly of an equal Height every where. Never before did I behold so just, so perfect a Resemblance to the Waves of the Ocean in the wintry Storm. When looking upon them and attentively considering their wild Order an Appearance, the Imagination is apt to say, these must once have been Liquid, and in that State when swelled to its greatest Agitation, suddenly congealed and made Solid by Power Omnipotent.*
>
> Thompson, a fur trader, writer, naturalist, cartographer, and explorer, was called Koo Koo Sint, which means "Star Gazer," by the Salish Flathead people for his habit of using the stars and planets to guide him. He journeyed approximately 90,000 kilometres and mapped 3.9 million square kilometres of central and western Canada over 34 years.
>
> An inveterate note-taker and writer, Thompson kept a journal recording his scientific and cultural observations for much of his life. He wrote over 101 notebooks. His observations have provided numerous insights into the fur trade, Aboriginal people, the geography of the West, his thoughts and feelings, and the role of women at the time, including the important role his wife, Charlotte Small, played in his work.
>
> In 1841, he used his survey calculations to complete an ambitious map of western Canada. This map, which measures 3.3 metres wide, was so accurate that cartographers used it as a foundation over the next century.

to their greatest agitation, it was all suddenly congealed and made solid by power omnipotent."

Thompson, whose evocative description marks the first words written about the valley in which Canmore now lies, journeyed to the Bow River in 1800. Led by North West Company trader Duncan McGillivray, he was on a reconnaissance mission seeking a pass over the Continental Divide to the Columbia Valley.

Even though Thompson and McGillivray went no further than Loder Peak, located east of Canmore, they were the first of many Euro-Canadians to enter the Bow Valley. Their arrival marked the beginning of the next period in the history of the Canmore Corridor. It was a time of transition that would transform the valley from an unexplored wilderness into a string of settlements.

The next group of Euro-Canadians would not arrive for another 32 years. Chief trader James Edward Harriott of the Hudson's Bay Company established Peigan Post in 1832 on what is now the Morley reserve. The post was closed just two years later.

As there is no proof that any of the Peigan Post employees travelled up the Bow Valley, the first European credited with visiting the site that would become the town of Canmore was a Métis free trader by the name of James Sinclair. In 1841, this University of Edinburgh-educated trader, whose mother was Cree and father was Scottish, led a group of 23 Métis families comprised of 121 individuals over the Continental Divide to the Oregon territory. The group entered the mountains via Devil's Gap and Lake Minnewanka, crossing into the Bow Valley via Carrot Creek Pass. (Carrot Creek Pass, located between Mount Peechee and Princess Margaret Mountain, was at one time a primary path into the Bow Valley. Today, however, Parks Canada discourages use of this route by hikers as it is part of an environmentally sensitive area). Once in the Bow Valley, Sinclair and his group followed the Bow River downstream until they stood opposite a narrow gap in the mountains. The pass, located high on the valley's south side, is known today as Whiteman's Gap. Abandoning their 55 clunky wood and leather Red River carts on the north side of the river, they coerced

Peigan Post (Old Bow Fort)

The fur trade had little direct effect on the Bow Valley, although the Stoney and other First Nations did benefit from trade goods brought into the region by the more northerly Cree.

Traders from the Hudson's Bay Company and the North West Company were focused on what is now northern Alberta, while the Americans had a brisk trade operation underway along the Missouri River. In 1832, the Hudson's Bay Company established Peigan Post on the Bow River, where they hoped to lure the Peigan away from trading with the American Fur Company.

The five-sided fort was surrounded by a high log palisade, and was situated on a high bluff overlooking the confluence of the Bow River and Old Fort Creek, located west of what is today the Morley townsite on the Stoney Nakoda reserve. Inside the stockade, traders built simple log homes; outside the walls, they constructed a trading hall attached to the fort known as the Indian House. Company employees exchanged a variety of goods such as axes, buttons, tobacco, ammunition, and rum, for over 5,000 furs in the first year alone.

While the first summer offered the promise of successful trading, the second summer was an anxious and dangerous time. The fort was badly damaged by fire in 1833 when it was left unattended. Chief trader James Edward Harriott recorded in his journal that "the Indians had burnt every bit of plank about the place and otherwise injured the building very much." He ordered his staff to repair the fort and, as a precaution, to build a bastion if attacked. Harriott began offering to trade only with the Peigan, but sending the Blood and Blackfoot to Fort Edmonton made the situation worse.

After Peigan camps around the fort were attacked by warring Blood, Harriott recognized that the Peigan trade would end, and the decision was made to close the post. On January 3, 1834, Hudson's Bay Company employees began to haul the trade goods and furs by dogsled to Fort Edmonton, and the fort was abandoned.

---

their 200 cattle across the water and struggled up the steep grade towards the distant pass.

It is unclear if the name Whiteman's Gap refers to Sinclair. Although his father was Scottish, Sinclair would not have identified himself as a white man given his Métis heritage.

It has been suggested that the name of the pass is connected to a pair of British spies, Lieutenant Henry James Warre, aide de camp to Charles Metcalfe, the governor of Canada at the time, and Lieutenant Mervin Vavasour, of the British Royal Engineers, who travelled over the pass in 1845. Posing as upper-class English gentlemen on a grand adventure, Warre and Vavasour had been sent by British Prime Minister Sir Robert Peel to investigate the Oregon territory, specifically its military capability, after President James K. Polk claimed that Oregon was, by right, part of the United States. The two men travelled with an entourage of nine Hudson's Bay Company employees, a number of horses, and all the accoutrements of the English upper crust, including fingernail brushes and fashionable clothing of the day such as beaver hats, frock coats, vests, and silk handkerchiefs. The spies and their escorts entered the Bow Valley following the same route Sinclair and his settlers took through Devil's Gap. Once at the confluence of the Bow Valley and Whiteman's Gap, the party camped to rest and prepare for the climb to the pass. While camping, Warre, an amateur artist, completed a few watercolour and pencil sketches of the picturesque valley, including a reproduction of the Bow Valley and its peaks at an undetermined location along the Bow River. The painting, *The Rocky Mountains near the Bow River*, features a

This 1848 composition by Henry Warre is the oldest known painting of the Canmore Corridor.

highly stylized image that could conceivably be the Three Sisters and the East End of Rundle. He made a second sketch on the following day, likely after the group had reached the pass. Warre later created a lithograph of a painting in his book *Sketches in North America and the Oregon Territory*, published in 1848, that depicts what is clearly Mount Rundle and Cascade Mountain. Of the three images, the lithograph of Mount Rundle and Cascade Mountain is immediately recognizable, and it is likely be the first painting depicting the Canmore Corridor section of the Bow Valley. Like Thompson, Warre was inspired by the scenery that lay before him.

Their route from the Bow Valley via Whiteman's Gap and the Spray Valley was treacherous, but as Warre described in *Sketches in North America and the Oregon Territory*, it was "grand in the extreme," even though the heat of the day, the cold of the night, and the biting and stinging of flies and mosquitoes tried their patience and stamina. "Our passage over the magnificent range of lofty mountains was not accomplished without much difficulty, and at a fearful sacrifice of the noble animals that aided us in the transport," Warre wrote. "The steepness of the mountain passes, the want of proper nourishment, the fearful falls that some of these animals sustained, rolling in some instances many hundred feet into the foaming torrent beneath, combined to cause this great loss."

Remarkably, within two months of the Warre-Vavasour party crossing the gap, a Belgian priest, Father Pierre-Jean De Smet achieved the same feat while on a peace mission involving the Blackfoot. As White Man Pass was named after De Smet, it is reasoned that Whiteman's Gap was also named after him. De Smet was guided by two Kootenay men whose ancestors had used the same route to reach the Plains for millennia. However, the men were reluctant to find their old enemies. They journeyed with a third Aboriginal man, who acted as an interpreter. The party travelled in the opposite direction of their predecessors; they first crossed White Man Pass. Here, De Smet erected a cross. He wrote in a letter to his superiors that this cross was "a sign of salvation and peace to all the scattered and itinerant tribes east and west of these gigantic and lurid mountains." After crossing White Man Pass, they hiked for three days through the Spray Valley, with its "enamelled meads [meadows], magnificent forests, and lakes in which the salmon-trout so abound," and where the "natural pyramids of the Rocky mountains seem to deride the artificial skill of man; they serve as a resting place for the clouds that come hither to seek repose, and to encircle their giant brows."

Father Pierre-Jean De Smet

De Smet found it wasn't all grand beauty, however. Like the journey Warre and Vavasour had previously undertaken, the going was tough, especially as they reached the mouth of the hanging valley of Whiteman's Gap. He wrote that it took his party six hours "to trace [the] route across fragments of broken rocks, through an extensive and parched forest and where millions of half consumed trees lay extended in every direction. Not a trace of vegetation remained, and never had I contemplated so dismal and destructive a conflagration!" According to De Smet's records, by the time they set up a small camp on the bank of the Bow River, both men and horses were battered and bruised. Instead of a peaceful evening nursing their wounds, they were filled with anxiety at the thought of spending the night at what De Smet's guides believed had once been a Blackfoot encampment. That night, De Smet's three companions had ominous dreams. One saw himself devoured by a bear, one saw "ravens and vultures, hovering over the heads of our father," and the other saw what De Smet described as "a bloody spectacle."

Even De Smet appeared to have felt some apprehension in the Bow Valley; he recorded in his journals that he had reached a land where there had been much bloodshed. Their fears, however, proved to be unfounded; the people who had previously camped at that spot were Stoney. De Smet met this group two days later near the spot where the Bow Valley meets the foothills. Like Sinclair, Warre, and Vavasour, De Smet did not spend much time in the Bow Valley. Once in the foothills, he headed north for Rocky Mountain House. His mission to secure peace with the Blackfoot eventually failed, but his writing indicates the discovery of exposed coal seams in the valleys of the Rocky Mountains and the Red Deer River Valley.

Other early adventurers, explorers, and prospectors were guided by De Smet's observations, but beyond his brief visit and his words, De Smet had no effect on the history of the Bow Valley. However, his contemporary, the Reverend Robert Rundle, a Wesleyan missionary who entered the Bow Valley in 1844 for a short visit as part of his work among the Stoney, had a notable effect on the Bow Valley's history. While in the valley, Rundle took a break from travelling to climb a mountain on the north side the Bow Valley. E.J. (Ted) Hart states in his book *The Place of Bows* that the mountain Rundle climbed was Grotto Mountain or one of its neighbours, rather than Mount Rundle, as is commonly believed.

Unlike Thompson, Rundle did not write about the grandeur of the Rockies from a perch high on the mountainside. Rundle's scramble was perhaps too adventurous for the gentle and unassuming Thompson, and as a result, Rundle provided the first account of a true mountain epic, an adventure that escalates out of control. "Am now climbing a mountain...," Rundle wrote. "I became quite ill thro' fatigue. But was in good spirits when climbing, until I was very high up. I made two attempts to get up an elevation but could not succeed. Rocks very steep—felt very weak, so weak, that at last I was near fainting whilst passing over a projecting layer of rock. I have some recollection of calling to the Almighty to assist me & praised by His name, my prayer was heard." Rundle made it

Exploration

Robert Rundle

Reverend Rundle

Reverend Robert Terrill Rundle, a Methodist missionary and Hudson's Bay Company chaplain, embodied the Wesleyan Methodist tradition of the wandering missionary. Even though Rundle had been posted to Fort Edmonton in 1840 and was expected to remain there to preach to company employees and Aboriginal people, an innate curiosity soon led him further afield.

Rundle spent eight years travelling through what was then known as Rupert's Land. He mingled freely with the Stoney, Cree, Assiniboine, and Blackfoot. His message found a receptive audience, including with the powerful Cree chief Maskepetoon, who, after befriending Rundle, set out to bring peace to the warring nations of what is now Alberta. This goal earned Maskepetoon the title "the Apostle of Peace." Rundle met the Stoney during a foray into the Bow Valley, who, like Maskepetoon, readily accepted Christianity and blended it with their own deep-rooted spiritual beliefs.

Just as the Cree and Stoney accepted his religion, Rundle accepted the Aboriginal people, who at first he admitted fearing. "What a contrast between my feelings now and on my first undertaking the journey to his wilderness. Then the thought of an Indian was almost accompanied with terror and dread but now my chief delight is to be with them," Rundle wrote in 1840.

Rundle returned home to England in 1848 for treatment of a broken arm that was not healing well, and he never returned to Canada. Mount Rundle, which overlooks Banff and extends east to Canmore, is named after him, as is Banff's Rundle Memorial United Church and a number of schools and subdivisions in Calgary and Edmonton.

safely down the mountain and back to his companions, who were camped on the valley floor, but not before experiencing what he referred to as a "fearful descent."

Rundle, who was quite taken with the Stoney and their easy acceptance of Christianity, returned to the Bow Valley in 1847 and held a service on June 27 for a small group of Stoney in the shadow of what later became known as Mount Rundle. As the spiritual beliefs of the Stoney were similar in principle to Christianity, they came to embrace this new religion as an extension of their own. They had no equivalent to Hell in their belief system, however, and therefore developed the concept of the "Bad Spirit's House." Even after Rundle left the Stoney in mid-summer 1847, they continued to practice their recently adopted religion while maintaining their own traditional belief system. Impressed by Rundle's obvious influence with the Stoney, James Hector named the distinctive mountain between Canmore and Banff after the priest.

As far as legacies and influences of early visitors to the Canmore Corridor go, few would have as much effect as the three-year Palliser Expedition. The purpose of this expedition was to evaluate the conditions on the southern prairies to determine if the area was suitable for settlement and agriculture and to probe the mountains for a suitable pass through to British Columbia. The idea of linking British Columbia with the rest of Canada was not new. The concept had been considered as early as the 1840s, but as the Hudson's Bay Company owned the drainage basin of Hudson Bay, a vast territory known as Rupert's Land, which included the Great Plains, building a railway would have been complicated. Plans to build a physical link across the prairies would have to wait. This did not mean, however, that Canada and Britain had to wait to begin the groundwork. The Royal Geographical Society of London, England, sent Irish landowner and explorer Captain John Palliser to British North America with a lofty mandate. At its heart, the society, and by extension Great Britain and the colonial government of Canada, wanted to affirm its ownership of Rupert's Land and the North West Territories. Settlement and

Captain John Palliser and geologist James Hector were members of the five-man Palliser expedition.

a road, perhaps even a railroad, near the border would help to accomplish that goal.

Members of the expedition led by Palliser included James Hector, a geologist and naturalist, Eugene Bourgeau, a botanist, John W. Sullivan, secretary and astronomical observer and magnetic observer, Lt. Thomas Blakiston, who had been assigned to measure the pull of the Earth's magnetic field, providing valuable geographical data, as the expedition travelled across the prairies.

After leaving Sault Ste Marie in 1857, the five men crossed the prairies and spent their first winter along the North Saskatchewan River. The following spring, Palliser followed the Kananaskis Valley in search of the pass that James Sinclair had used on his sojourn through the Rockies. Sinclair had shared his knowledge with Palliser, providing the Irish explorer with information he would need to find the pass Palliser would come to call Kananaskis Pass, after Kananaskis, a native man, who survived an axe blow to the head, and Palliser was determined to find it. The expedition's botanist, Eugene Bourgeau, spent his time travelling between Lac des Arcs and Cascade Mountain gathering plant specimens and naming mountains, including Pigeon Mountain, Windy Mountain (now Mount Lougheed), and Heart Mountain. Bourgeau and Hector also named Grotto Mountain. Beyond the names these scientists and explorers bestowed on the features of the Canmore Corridor, they brought scientific exploration to the region.

Hector camped at Indian Flats for three days and wandered along the valley floor and slopes, sketching, collecting fossils, and writing. "Just opposite our camp there is a mountain with three peaks which form a striking group, while further up the valley there is a cross valley or nick bounded by a very lofty precipice," he wrote, describing Whiteman's Gap. Hector and his small party left the Canmore Corridor on August 15, 1858. They continued west, following the Bow River past Cascade Mountain. Their journey would then take them over Vermilion Pass, down into the Kootenay Valley, and over another pass to the Beaverfoot River, which led him to the Kicking Horse River. He eventually followed the Bow River to its headwater at Bow Lake before carrying on to Fort Edmonton.

Hector returned to the Bow Valley in August 1859, where he once again camped at familiar spots at Lac des Arcs and Indian Flats. As Hector continued exploration beyond the Canmore Corridor,

Exploration

another Scot, James Carnegie, the ninth Earl of Southesk, headed southeast, bound for Old Bow Fort, as the site of Peigan Post had become known. Their paths crossed in the Pipestone Valley on September 26, 1859, when Southesk discovered a camp used by Hector and a nearby tree where the young explorer and naturalist had recorded: *Exploring Expedition. Aug. 23, 1859. Dr. Hector.*

Southesk, 32 at the time, was in the Rocky Mountains on an extended holiday. Following the advice of his doctor, Southesk

Earl of Southesk

Born in Edinburgh in 1827, James Carnegie, the ninth Earl of Southesk, was the first "tourist" to pass through the Canmore Corridor. Southesk grew up in privileged surroundings of Kinnaird Castle, his family's ancestral home. In 1859, after the death of his first wife and following the advice of his doctor, he took an extended holiday to the Rocky Mountains for fresh air and sport. Although dressed in traditional Western buckskin, he was accompanied by an entourage that included a gamekeeper from his Scottish estate and an Iroquois cook.

Today, a lake, a pass, and a mountain are named in his honour and native artifacts collected on his trip are on display at the Royal Alberta Museum.

The Earl of Southesk could be considered the first tourist to visit the Canmore corridor.

had come to the mountains for fresh air and sport. The nature of mountain travel and hunting disappointed him, however. He described the desolation of the mountains with harsh words that mirrored his experiences. "The very mass and vastness of the mountains depress and daunt the soul; scarcely can you look up at the blue sky without some portentous object sternly frowning-down your gaze," he wrote in his journals, which were published in 1875 as *Saskatchewan and the Rocky Mountains: A diary and narrative of sport, and adventure, during a journey through the Hudson's Bay Company's territories in 1859 and 1860.*

Even though he described leaving the Rockies, on the first of October, as a "greater joy" than entering them (a month earlier), Southesk still found beauty in the Canmore Corridor, which he called "a pretty vale" where the Bow River "winds through ... in a deep, still, dark blue current, and forms numerous shallow lakes alongside its courts, which are separated from the stream, sometimes by reedy flats, sometimes by low wooded banks." Southesk also commented on fire-charred pines of great stature, 10 to 12 feet in girth, growing in the valley and the visibly lower mountains than those seen in the north, writing that they "continue to lessen in height at each succeeding great bend of the river, but their rocky character remains unchanged."

Two years after Southesk passed through the valley, travelling from west to east, a party of six Overlanders, a term used to refer to men who travelled across Canada to the goldfields of British Columbia, reached the Bow River in the fall of 1861. Led by Dr. Alexander P. Reid, the group was attempting to reach the gold-rich Fraser River. Guided by an Assiniboine Métis, Baptiste Gabriel, Reid and his party left Edmonton on September 2, 1861. Gabriel deserted the party eleven days after leaving Edmonton. The remaining Overlanders were left to find their own way to the Bow Valley, and they accomplished this goal a few days later. Once in the valley, two of the men travelled 24 kilometres upstream in search of the North Kananaskis Pass. Although they were unable to find the pass, they managed to find and hire a new guide who led them up the Bow Valley to Castle Mountain and into the Columbia Valley via Vermilion Pass.

Meanwhile, by 1869, the Union Pacific Railroad had completed the first transcontinental railway in North America. One year later, as a way to stave off American interest in the North-West Territories, the Hudson's Bay Company sold Rupert's Land to the Canadian government for £300,000. British Columbia joined Confederation in 1871. This decision was partly based on a promise made by the federal government to build a transcontinental railway. In 1880, led by Prime Minister John A. Macdonald, the Canadian government finally announced firm plans to build a railway extending from one end of the new country to another. It was an audacious plan for a country that was not even four years old and that had a total population of only 3.5 million. Alexander Mackenzie, leader of the Liberal Party, described it as "insane recklessness." The Liberals believed a railway line that looped south into the United States and then up into Manitoba would make more sense, as it would remove the challenge of crossing the Canadian Shield.

Regardless of whether the idea was insane, Macdonald intended to build an all-Canadian route. The information collected by Southesk, the members of the Palliser Expedition, the missionaries, and the fur trade explorers formed a record, some of it illustrated by drawings and maps, that would provide the Canadian Pacific Railway (CPR) with reference material as it set out to choose a route for the transcontinental railway. The CPR's chief engineer, Sir Sandford Fleming, even ensured that his surveyors had copies of Southesk's book.

Fleming took charge of the Canadian Pacific Survey in 1871, and by mid-summer he had 800 men surveying potential routes for the railroad. By the end of 1876, the CPR had considered six passes through the Rocky Mountains and a total of twelve routes across the country. It appears, based on Fleming's 1877 report, that his surveyors did not investigate or give much thought to the Bow Valley or Kicking Horse Pass.

The History of Canmore

The botanist John Macoun camped throughout the Bow Valley in the early 1870s.

The botanist on Fleming's expedition, John Macoun, did explore the Bow Valley. He investigated the flora and fauna of the Canmore Corridor and along the Bow Valley as far west as Castle Mountain.

Fleming, meanwhile, continued to champion the Yellow Head Pass west of Jasper. He believed this pass was a good fit for the railway as construction would be easier and less costly due to the relatively low height and gentle gradient of the pass. "Accordingly, the Yellow Head Pass was, for the time, selected, and further surveys through the main mountain range, by the Howse Pass, and other passes in a more southern latitude, were abandoned ... It is, however, undoubtedly established that the main Rocky Mountain chain can be crossed with ease by the Yellow Head Pass," wrote Fleming.

For a period of time, the Canadian government agreed with Fleming, and it appeared that the Bow Valley and the Canmore Corridor would be disregarded. On Feb. 15, 1881, however, CPR syndicate officials met in St. Paul, Minnesota and made the surprising decision to route the rail line through the Bow Valley and Kicking Horse Pass. Macoun's favourable report on the potential for agriculture in what is now southern Alberta may have helped the CPR decide upon the southern route. Ultimately though, this decision, which was rooted more in politics than practicality, determined the destiny of the Canmore Corridor.

The industrial age was about to reach the Canmore Corridor, and the peace, tranquility, and even the difficult travel conditions that the Aboriginal people, fur traders, explorers, scientists, missionaries, and of course the Earl of Southesk, the valley's first tourist, had experienced was about to end. Although the surveyors travelled with more men and equipment than any other group who had previously entered the Bow Valley, they were still light on the land compared to the noisy beast that was about to arrive: the railhead. Soon, screeching locomotives hauling railcars stacked high with supplies, and smoke, steam, and cinders would reach the Bow Valley, accompanied by hundreds of men and horses and the sound of ringing steel would fill the air.

3 Railway

In 1881, when the CPR made its historic decision to cross the Canadian Rockies by way of the Bow Valley and Kicking Horse Pass, the route had not been officially surveyed. The company employed engineer and surveyor Major A.B. Rogers, a famously taciturn American, to find a route from the Bow Valley through the Selkirk Mountains, a section of the much larger Columbia Mountains that border the Rocky Mountains to the west. The CPR reasoned that if a feasible route could not be found through the Selkirk Mountains, then the route would follow the Columbia River as it dipped south. This would add length and expense to the project, which by this time was well underway and rapidly moving west towards Calgary.

Even though the southern route through the Bow Valley presented many challenges, it also offered several advantages over the more northern Yellowhead Pass route that had been proposed. Most importantly, it would be shorter and faster to build. It would also prevent the Americans from building spur lines from the Northern Pacific Railroad north into Canada. Building the line on the southern route also ensured that the government could send troops to the border if the United States became aggressive. Time was also of the essence, to ensure British Columbia remained part of Canada. Without the railway, the fledgling province had little reason to remain committed to Canada.

And if speed was the order of the day, Rogers was more than happy to comply. Born in Massachusetts in 1829, Rogers was a slight man with an astonishing fortitude and drive that allowed him to live on hardtack (dried crackers) and chewing tobacco. He was determined, frugal, temperamental, relentless, and not motivated by money in the slightest. The $5,000 bonus the CPR was offering for completing the survey was meaningless to Rogers. All the motivation the thorny surveyor needed was a promise that his name be attached to the pass through the Selkirk Mountains.

Rogers also possessed a remarkable ability to swear, and with his piercing blue eyes and massive, stark-white sideburns, he struck the men working for him as a frightening figure. But behind his thick armour, Rogers had a soft spot for reliable people, such as his young nephew Albert Rogers, who first called Canmore's snow-covered Three Sisters the "Three Nuns," and the legendary Banff packer and guide Tom Wilson.

In the summer of 1882, after Rogers reached the pass that would eventually bear his name, his attention turned to surveying the Bow Valley. He established a base camp near the confluence of the Bow and Kananaskis rivers, just southwest of Old Bow Fort. The camp, anchored by a small log storehouse, became known as Padmore, which was named for the CPR assistant commissioner Paddy Padmore, who had developed a profound love for the mountains. Although the site was abandoned in 1885, Padmore is considered the Bow Valley's first permanent settlement.

The arrival of the surveyors to the Bow Valley signalled the end of a 23-year-long interlude of peace and solitude that harkened back to the days before the members of the Palliser Expedition had explored the region in 1858. Aside from the presence of a handful of prospectors such as Joe Healy, who is believed to have used Whiteman's Gap to cross through to the Spray Valley in 1863 and again in 1874, the valley had remained as remote and unknown as it had been before European and Canadian explorers arrived with their economic and scientific interests. At this time, the only significant non-Aboriginal presence was at Morley, where the McDougall family had established a Methodist mission in 1873.

In 1882, Major A.B. Rogers led a survey party through the Bow Valley and across the Kicking Horse Pass.

The survey party assembled by Rogers numbered around 100 men, most of whom had reached the abandoned fort by travelling north from Fort Benton, Montana. They arrived with 80 pack animals and 8 wagons loaded with supplies for the season. The party included engineers, axemen, chainmen, levellers, transitmen, and packers. They slept in tents and tipis, and survived on the barest of provisions, such as bannock, beans, and bacon, and

Grand Trunk Pacific Railway

Although the CPR eventually chose a route through the Bow Valley and over Kicking Horse Pass for their rail line, Sir Sandford Fleming's favoured route, the more northerly Yellowhead Pass, was later used by the Grand Trunk Pacific Railway. Beginning in Winnipeg and terminating on the west coast at Prince Rupert, this rail line was completed in 1914. Construction crews reached the Continental Divide in 1911, with workers housed at Summit City, west of present day Jasper. The rail line over the Yellowhead Pass is used today by Canada's only transcontinental passenger service. As North America's lowest elevation crossing of the Continental Divide, it also has a competitive advantage over the CPR line for hauling freight.

The town of Jasper grew from a railway siding along the Grand Trunk Pacific Railway.

wore heavy boots and inadequate coats. Photographs of Rogers's surveyors taken in the Kicking Horse Pass show lean, sturdy men with serious, drawn faces.

On July 15, 1881, two weeks behind schedule and with a furious desire to begin work, Rogers sent one group of surveyors up the Kananaskis Valley to investigate Palliser's pass, now known as North Kananaskis Pass, while the rest of the surveyors were sent west along the Bow River. Rogers was worried about his nephew, whom he had left near Kicking Horse Pass in his hurry to rendezvous at Old Bow Fort. He left the surveyors to their work and, accompanied by Tom Wilson and a few other men, raced for Kicking Horse Pass to rendezvous with the starving and exhausted Albert.

The survey team assigned to the Bow Valley was led by a reconnaissance team tasked with surveying the valley floor to record landforms, minerals, and bodies of water. With compass and aneroid barometer in hand, the reconnaissance team measured distance, direction, and altitude. They left blazes cut into trees, pickets, or stone piles to mark their route and kept a journal of detailed descriptions of the terrain on either side of the proposed line.

The axemen followed the reconnaissance team and cleared a 70-metre-wide strip of ground, in order to provide a clear path and line of sight for the two chainmen. The task of the chainmen was to drive survey stakes into the ground at 30-metre intervals and then link them with heavy steel wire. After the chain had been laid out, an engineer plotted a precise line on a map. Finally, the leveller established the grade of the line. The work for all members of the party was difficult and the wages were low. The lowly axemen and packers earned just $30 a month and the engineer, who was the best paid, received up to $160, a very good wage at that time.

As the surveyors slowly made their way west up the Bow Valley from Padmore, they pushed through dense forests choked with deadfall, thick bushes (the kind that drive bushwhackers mad), bug-infested swamps, an undulating river filled with ice-cold water, freezing rain, hot sun, and rough, rocky ground. The party was expected to be on the move at every hour of the day and under every climatic condition imaginable while also enduring a litany of hardships such as scurvy, snow blindness, frostbite, heat stroke, injury, forest fire, and insects.

The first major obstacle the survey crew encountered was the narrow entrance to the Bow Valley, known appropriately as

Anthracite

Anthracite, located between Canmore and Banff, was the Bow Valley's first official town. It was founded in 1883 by the Cascade Coal Company. Anthracite was a stereotypical frontier town and had seven saloons, a brothel, two hotels, boarding houses to accommodate single miners, a church, a post office, a doctor's office, three general stores, a pool hall, and a bakery.

The town was first officially surveyed in 1888; the site was divided into 337 lots between the CPR line and the Cascade River. The mine entrance itself was just north of the rail line and the commercial buildings ran parallel to the south side of the line.

One of Anthracite's most infamous visitors was Ernest Cashel, a young man originally from Wyoming wanted for the murder of a Lacombe rancher. Cashel had decided to hang his hat in Anthracite and had barely checked into a boarding house on January 24, 1903, when he was promptly arrested by a vigilant police officer, Constable Blythe, a member of the NWMP. Cashel escaped police custody shortly after his arrest with the aid of his brother. However, Cashel was once again arrested, and this time he was hung for murder. It was men like Cashel who prompted owners of the Bow Valley coal mines to request that the national government station members of the NWMP in the Bow Valley mining camps.

As a mining town, Anthracite's fortune hung on the success of the coal mine, which proved to be tenuous at best. While the NWMP served to keep the peace, there was nothing they could do regarding finding a market for the coal. The CPR balked at buying Anthracite's coal, which was more expensive than the coal available at Lethbridge's mine.

The town's riverside location was prone to flooding, which further added to the community's woes. The first major flood occurred in 1894; it destroyed bridges and several buildings. The flood of June 16, 1897, flooded the mines and drowned horses and mules used to haul coal cars. The 1897 flood also destroyed houses and commercial businesses.

the Bow River Gap, or simply The Gap. In a 1905 CPR tourist brochure, *The Challenge of the Mountains*, the writer eloquently describes The Gap as the entrance to the Canadian Rockies. "It seems that the train has reached an impasse, and that there is no way by which it can surmount the lordly line of heights drawn up across its path. But suddenly, it takes a sharp turn, finds itself between two walls of vertical rock, and a passage is forced to the world of mountains beyond. It has found and followed the course

---

Coal production reached a high of 100,000 tons in 1893, but overpriced coal, flooding, and the challenging geography of the Bow Valley led to a sharp drop in production. By 1903, only 5,185 tons of coal were extracted from Anthracite's mine.

The Canadian Anthracite Coal Company, which had bought the operation from the Cascade Coal Company in 1885, officially abandoned Anthracite on June 30, 1904. Most of Anthracite's buildings were then moved to other Bow Valley communities, including Canmore.

Looking northeast across Anthracite in the 1890s.

Today, very little remains of Anthracite, although determined visitors will find concrete and steel relics scattered throughout the forest and open meadows south of the Trans-Canada Highway, approximately three kilometres east of the Banff interchange.

of the Bow..." But given the crew's task and speed, The Gap and the rest of the Canmore Corridor would not have been any more scenically significant than any other spot along the survey line.

The entire survey crew needed to work at a feverish pace to stay ahead of rail line construction. The end of the track was bound for Calgary and moving quickly. Thousands of workers, including Chinese labourers, along with hundreds of horses laboured at

Holt City (now known as Lake Louise) was a construction camp along the rail line.

the task of building the railway. Sixty-five railcars ferried supplies along the completed section, while further back along the line, came the support train with its large, three-story high boarding cars that provided dormitories on the two top levels and kitchens and dining rooms on the first level for teamsters, tracklayers, blacksmiths and carpenters and smaller freight and passenger cars that provided space for offices and workshops.

By mid-August 1883, after passing through Calgary, construction crews set their sights on the mountains. The daily routine for railway construction crews was efficient and well orchestrated. Trains, each hauling rails, ties, and telegraph poles, moved westward to the end of track. At this point, supplies were unloaded on either side of the line and then loaded onto wagons hauled by teams of horses. The ties went down first, followed by the rails and then the fasteners, screws, and spikes. It was fast, difficult, and demanding work, but it paid well, and good tracklayers could earn up to $2.50 a day, double what other railway labourers would make.

The rail line reached Padmore on August 25, 1883. Construction then continued westward toward The Gap and eventually reached Siding 27, now Canmore, in the fall of 1883. The CPR built sidings, which featured a short secondary section of track with railway stations every 11 to 32 miles along the main line, including at Kananaskis and The Gap. Construction continued through the Bow Valley and reached Holt City (which was renamed Laggan, but is now known as Lake Louise) before winter set in. The CPR re-designated Siding 27, or Canmore, as a divisional point, which meant more locomotives and larger work crews were needed at this location. Divisional points, which featured locomotive maintenance, repair and refuelling facilities, were built every 200 kilometres, the distance a wood-burning locomotive could travel before it required refuelling.

The first scheduled train, pulled by a slat-burning locomotive, passed through Canmore on May 11, 1884, at noon sharp. Beyond Siding 27, the CPR completed construction of its rail line through the treacherously steep Kicking Horse Pass. The east- and westbound railheads were joined at Craigellachie, British Columbia. It was here on November 7, 1885, that CPR executive Sir Donald Smith drove the railway's last spike.

Although Canmore became a thriving mining community in the last decade of the 1800s, its importance as a railway town officially came to an end in 1898 with the introduction of new, more efficient and powerful locomotives. With these new locomotives, the CPR could increase the distance between its divisional points. As a result, the CPR closed the Canmore depot and moved its facilities and employees to Calgary and what is now Lake Louise.

After the railway workers had been relocated, Canmore's first neighbourhood began to languish. Before long, it ceased to exist entirely. Many of the original homes and businesses were demolished (including the one-room schoolhouse, the water tower and coal chute), left to rot, or moved, as was the section house. Built in 1883 for the divisional point foreman, the section house was moved to 5th Street. It was later torn down. Within a few years, only two houses remained and those were eventually demolished, as well. Canmore's original railway station was the only commercial building to survive. Once located near what is now The Hostel Bear, it was demolished in the 1960s.

The Naming of Canmore

Siding 27 was officially named Canmore in 1884. For many years, it was accepted that Sir Donald Smith (Lord Strathcona), a director of the CPR, named Canmore after a Scottish king. However, no evidence has been found to date that links Smith to the name Canmore. Instead, the origin of the name is likely more ordinary than is often believed. When choosing names for stations and depots such as Canmore, the CPR relied on its land commissioner John McTavish, to provide a list of place names for each new stop along the rail line. Therefore, it can be assumed that the name came into being simply because it was on a list of possibilities provided by the land commissioner.

The land commissioner McTavish would have been familiar with the name Canmore from Scottish history. The word is an anglicized version of Máel Coluim mac Donnchada, a name that means "big head" or "great chief." The name had originally been given to Malcolm III, who reigned as Scotland's king from 1058 to 1093.

4 Growth

As the tracklayers continued their journey westward, other workers remained at each newly established siding to build the infrastructure needed to service locomotives and house workers. At Siding 27, this development took place on the broad flats north of what would become known as Policeman's Creek. This railway settlement was the nucleus of Canmore as we know it today.

Within a year of the rail line arriving in the Bow Valley, Siding 27 had been renamed Canmore and the site had been transformed from raw wilderness to a small but busy railway divisional point and settlement. By the spring of 1884, barely a year after construction of the rail line had been completed up to the confluence of the Bow and Spray valleys, the CPR had completed the infrastructure required for the divisional and layover facilities. The infrastructure, which was clustered around the main line and a two-track siding, included a roundhouse, a large maintenance shed, a water tower, and a fuel yard. The 12-bay roundhouse, used to store and service locomotives, had 12 sets of tall double doors and faced south, where it overlooked the turntable. The roundhouse was built by CPR carpenters, and the construction was supervised by engineer P. Turner Bone during the winter of 1883–84. The roundhouse was constructed following the same plans used to build the Gleichen roundhouse, located at a divisional point east of Calgary. The long maintenance shed was built to the immediate east of the roundhouse.

Crews erected a water tower and established a large yard for storing the wood needed to fuel the steam locomotives. Once the locomotives began using coal, a tall coal chute was built on the north side of the tracks near the water tower. A siding extended from the rail line on the west of the depot. Beyond the siding, an old boxcar, staffed by agent Charles Compton, initially served as the railway station. The boxcar was replaced by a permanent station in the summer of 1884. It was built to William Cornelius Van Horne's specifications in order to ensure that it looked identical to other stations along the CPR. The new station, directly

Growth

Locomotives were stored and serviced in the roundhouse.

across the tracks from the roundhouse, included a freight shed, an office, and a waiting room. On the second floor was a small two-bedroom apartment for the station agent. During the initial phase of railway infrastructure development at Siding 27, railway surveyors also laid out a simple grid of streets north of the tracks. Section Avenue faced the tracks and—from west to east—Young, Sidney, Mountain, William, and Jones streets ran north of Section Avenue towards Mount Lady Macdonald. Howard Street closed the grid to the north, which created five rough town blocks.

By 1886, a commercial district of sorts stood along Section Avenue facing the tracks, as early entrepreneurs began to build businesses that offered services to the railway workers living in Canmore and loggers based in logging camps located throughout the Canmore Corridor and the nearby Spray Valley. The businesses later began offering services to coal miners. Section Avenue was the only street that formed according to the CPR survey plan. The buildings were rough and for the most part hastily built structures—with the exception of the railway facilities and one or two stores. A mix of hand-hewn log shacks and sod houses stood alongside one- and two-storey clapboard buildings constructed with locally milled wood.

The History of Canmore

Growth

In 1886, Canmore was centred on the rail line.

The History of Canmore

Most businesses were designed in an early Western style, with square false fronts that rose to the peak of the roof. These buildings had a large, clean facade and created a sense of prosperity and an urban feel, which hid their coarseness. Even the smallest stores, which were little more than small shacks, had false fronts. Early Canmore businesses included S.C. Vick's watchmaking business, E.L. Smith and Co., which sold hardware and tinware and MacNulty Brothers General Store. Bill Coffee built an eatery to the west of the roundhouse. Next door to Coffee's establishment was the section house, which provided a home for the section foreman.

Records show that Canmore's first boarding house was Mountain House, which opened for business in 1885. The boarding house, owned and operated by Mr. and Mrs. James Conroy and their daughter Mary, was across the rail line from the roundhouse and the maintenance sheds. The two-storey clapboard building, which had a peaked roof, brick chimneys on each end, and white-framed windows, was one of the largest structures in Canmore at the time. The Conroys advertised their business by painting "Mountain House" in large white capital letters on three sides of the building. Mary and another woman who moved to Canmore

Mountain House welcomed its first guests in 1885.

Growth

The Hansen family beside their boxcar home in the mid-1880s.

with the Conroys, a Miss Foley, are believed to be the first young women to live in Canmore, and in a new town filled with men, they would have been very popular.

Joseph Chenier and Co., which opened in 1885, was a small grocery store that first operated from the basement of Mountain House. In 1888, when his business began to prosper, Chenier, who also served as Canmore's postmaster, moved his operation to a nearby building. In 1891, his young wife passed away, leaving him to raise their three-month-old son, Hermand.

Most railway workers were housed in converted boxcars hauled from the tracks on two short spur lines; one line ran south from the water tower and the other faced Section Avenue. The boxcar accommodations were small but they appear to have been relatively comfortable, according to photographs housed at the Glenbow Museum in Calgary of J.P. Hansen, a CPR gang foreman and his wife and daughter inside their boxcar home. Each boxcar had a row of narrow windows and all the basic comforts, including a stove, a table, beds, and wooden chairs.

By the late 1880s, Canmore began to expand beyond the surveyed grid. A haphazard collection of houses and businesses were constructed south of the roundhouse, towards the river.

5 Prospecting

Following the arrival of CPR crews, prospectors began finding their way into the Bow Valley. They would draw on accounts such as Pierre Jean De Smet's 1840s reference to coal and other minerals. The amount of prospecting increased dramatically when railway workers also began prospecting as a way to increase their meagre wage.

Two prospectors, known today only by their last names of French and Marsh, discovered and staked a seam of coal above the Bow River high on the north-facing slope of Wind Ridge six kilometres east of what is now Canmore. Their operation, which became known as Marsh Mine, comprised two primitive tunnels driven horizontally into the upper of two distinct coal seams.

Brothers Tom and William McCardell and their friend Frank McCabe were railway workers who stumbled upon the mineral hot springs that eventually led to creation of what is today Banff National Park. While they attempted to lay a claim to the hot springs, other parties also claimed ownership, leading the federal government to take control of the land instead, establishing a 26-square-kilometre reserve around the hot springs. Although this particular discovery is their best-known legacy, William McCardell and McCabe also staked a number of mineral claims east of Banff; in 1884, they stumbled upon an exposed coal seam in the drainage containing Whiteman's Creek (known today as Canmore Creek). The coal samples McCardell and McCabe sent for testing confirmed that the valley around Siding 27 held high-quality semi-anthracite coal that was made of more than 87 percent fixed carbon. This means that it burned with an almost flameless glow and generated practically no smoke.

McCardell later partnered with Bow Valley coal miners, Albert Grainger Sr. and Joe Sedlock, to form the Grainger Collieries, which later bought the Marsh Mine and added to other claims the three men held in the valley. They eventually sold their entire operation to the Canmore Coal Company in 1928.

Early prospectors also opened a small gold mine high on the slopes of Ha Ling Peak; it is believed that they teased some gold

How Coal Forms

Over 150 million years ago, during the late Jurassic and Lower Cretaceous periods, when dinosaurs ruled the earth and birds, mammals, and flowering plants were just beginning to emerge, the Bow Valley was covered by vast tropical swamps. In these swamps, plant material collected in thick peat bogs, which were subsequently covered by layers of sand, dirt, and dust. As sediment built up over the peat bogs, heat and pressure over great periods of time compressed the organic material. This process slowly changed the plant matter into coal.

Folding and faulting is obvious in this outcrop along Three Sisters Drive.

Like wine, coal improves with age, as long as heat and pressure are present. Hard, lustrous anthracite coal, the highest grade of coal, spent the greatest amount of time under the right pressure. Then, around 70 million years ago, two plates of the Earth's crust collided violently and crumpled upwards to create the Rocky Mountains. Layers of sediment that had formed coal seams over millions of years were folded, squeezed, and twisted. In the Bow Valley, older strata were pushed on top of younger, which forced sections of coal seams both above and below other layers of rock. Around 65 million years ago, the general form of mountain contours in the Canadian Rockies was in place; coal seams were scattered through the Bow Valley at different angles and sandwiched between rock strata.

Three basic forms of coal exist. Anthracite coal is high in carbon and low in oxygen and hydrogen and thus produces a hot, smokeless flame. This makes anthracite coal ideal for heating and steam generation. It is also the least common form of coal. Semi-anthracite coal is also relatively uncommon; this type of coal is ideal for steam generation and was mined in the Bow Valley. Finally, bituminous metallurgical coal is a lower grade of coal. Because it spent less time under pressure, it is lower in carbon and higher in oxygen and hydrogen, which makes it well-suited for conversion to coke and therefore suitable for the steel industry.

and profit out of the rock at the surface. They found very little gold below the surface, however, and the mine was quickly abandoned.

The mandate for CPR surveyors had been to find a route for the rail line, and prospectors hungered for gold and silver, but geologist George Mercer Dawson came to the area for different reasons. He was sent to the Bow Valley in 1883 as part of the Geological Survey of Canada with a mandate to catalogue minerals along the newly completed CPR. While others had claimed coal seams that had been exposed at the ground's surface, no one realized the extent of the Bow Valley coal measures, or deposits, until the survey party completed its work in 1885, referring to his discovery as the Cascade Coal Basin.

"In connection with the work in this part of the Rocky Mountains, the existence has been proved of large tracts of coal-bearing Cretaceous rocks in the very heart of the range, of which the Anthracite region of the Cascade River is a special development ... As this portion of the mountains is at present attracting much attention, in consequence of the proximity of the railway, and the maps now existing are quite unserviceable, it is proposed to publish the information now in hand, in the form of a preliminary map. This will serve as a guide to prospectors and others, and may eventually form the basis for a more complete map as the surveys progress," Dawson wrote in the summary report for the years 1884 and 1885.

As part of subsequent reports, Dawson produced a highly detailed geological map of the Bow Valley's portion of the Cascade Coal Basin that indicated the edges of the basin and the locations of the operating coal mines, including the Marsh Mine, which is referred to as Marsh's Mine on Dawson's map, located six kilometres east of Canmore and the mine at Anthracite opened by the Cascade Coal Company in the fall of 1883, four kilometres east of the Banff siding.

The Cascade Coal Basin was a 50-kilometre-long bed of coal covering over 150 square kilometres. It extended from the Kananaskis River in the east to Cascade Mountain in the west and was three kilometres wide on average. The basin was eventually discovered to be part of a much larger coal bed that stretched 80 kilometres north from the Bow Valley to the Red Deer River and beyond into the Foothills. The coal bed ran parallel to the Canadian Rockies and extended up to 30 kilometres eastward.

The basin was found to hold both semi-anthracite coal and low-volatile bituminous coal in at least 12 seams. Dawson noted that many portions of the seams appeared to be in "a shattered and slickensided state," but also stated "the prospects for profitable mining on a large scale appear to be in general very favourable."

In 1914, the Commission of Conservation estimated that the Cascade Coal Basin contained 404 million tons of anthracite coal and 1,212 million tons of softer grades, such as bituminous coal. Even though Dawson did not file his official report until 1885, the value of the Cascade Coal Basin was recognized in 1884 when the

George Dawson

Dr. George Mercer Dawson, born in Pictou, Nova Scotia, in 1849, is regarded as one of Canada's finest scientists. He studied geology and paleontology at London's Royal School of Mines before returning to Canada to begin one of the most comprehensive geological surveys of western Canada ever undertaken.

Officially, Dawson was sent to the Bow Valley by the Canadian government as part of the Geological Survey of Canada to catalogue minerals along the newly completed Canadian Pacific Railway. Through 1883 and 1884, he compiled a report that detailed extensive coal deposits, but he also used his time to better understand the geological nature of the Rocky Mountains and officially map peaks such as Mount Temple and Mount Assiniboine.

Dawson is best known for making Canada's first official dinosaur discovery, although it was one of his assistants, Joesph Tyrrell, who actually found the bones in the Red Deer River Valley. Dawson also mapped what is now the Yukon Territory (Dawson City is named in his honour) and was appointed director of the Geological Survey of Canada in 1895.

Dawson suffered from a lifelong affliction known as Pott's disease. The disease stunted his growth and created a hump in his back, which makes his extensive travels through western Canada even more impressive.

The History of Canmore

Canmore was a remote railway siding when the full extent of coal deposits was revealed by Dawson's survey work in the mid 1880s.

Department of the Interior established the 9,234-hectare Cascade Coal District. Land within the district was leased, and landowners had the option to convert their holdings to freehold title at a minimum cost of $10 per 0.4 hectares for the less valuable bituminous coal lands. Any lands that contained anthracite deposits would cost $20 per acre.

Given that coal was a valuable commodity, the Cascade Coal Basin represented vast wealth for mining companies and the Government of Canada. As a result, Canmore's future in 1884, just one year after the rail line had been completed through the Bow Valley, looked bright.

6 Mining

For the first few years of its existence, in the mid-1880s, Canmore was strictly a railway town. Coal mining, which would become Canmore's lifeblood, was already underway at the Marsh Mine, but it was a small operation six kilometres east of Canmore, located high on the north-facing slope of Wind Ridge.

As construction of the rail line through the Bow Valley was being completed in 1883, the valley's first formal mining company, Cascade Coal Co., claimed 180 hectares at the confluence of Devil's Head Creek and the Bow River, between what are now the towns of Canmore and Banff. Like coal from the Marsh Mine, coal produced by the Cascade Coal Co. was sold locally for heating and cooking. Southwest of the Cascade Coal Co.'s mine, a man known only as Captain Hughes opened another seam on the Black Diamond Property in 1884, along the creek flowing from Johnson Lake. The rest of the land in the Cascade Coal Basin was quickly staked by prospectors and entrepreneurs.

The Cascade Coal Co. halted work during the winter of 1883–84, shortly after the rails were laid down along the base of Cascade Mountain, but as the mine owners were not certain they could compete against Pennsylvania coal, by the summer of 1884, they had decided to put the mine up for sale, which opened the door for a group of Canadian and American businessmen who would play an important role in the future of Canmore.

John and McLeod Stewart (the mayor of Ottawa, Ontario, from 1887 to 1888), who were later joined by their brother Archibald Stewart, were the leaders of this group of businessmen. They bought the Cascade Coal Co. and immediately began negotiating with the CPR to secure favourable shipping rates. William Cornelius Van Horne, the CPR's general manager and later president, agreed to provide rates that were low enough to allow the Cascade Coal Co. to compete in markets beyond the Calgary region.

With burgeoning optimism, the Stewarts published a prospectus in 1885 that outlined their plans and holdings. By this time, the Cascade Coal Co. held 550 hectares of land with mineral rights. The land was thought to contain 20.3 million tons of recoverable coal; it was estimated that the coal would cost $1.50 per ton to mine and would yield a profit of $5 per ton. Based on positive evaluations of the mine, the coal it contained, and the confidence of the Stewarts, the Stewarts' partners and a few new investors agreed to form a syndicate.

Once the syndicate had gained control of McCardell and McCabe's 1884 claim on Whiteman's Creek, they incorporated the Canadian Anthracite Coal Co. and received a royal charter from Queen Victoria on October 28, 1886. The charter gave the company permission to mine coal in Canmore and to develop its lease lands as the directors saw fit. With the charter in hand, the Canadian Anthracite Coal Co. opened the No. 1 Mine—Canmore's first coal mine—in 1887.

The No.1 Mine and the coal mine at Anthracite near Banff held great promise for the Canadian Anthracite Coal Co., as both proved to contain the high quality semi-anthracite coal. The No 1. Mine was also relatively easy to mine, as its seams were thicker and more uniform than the mine in Anthracite. It was also relatively free of thrust faults, which occur where one layer of rock was pushed up and onto another layer of rock during mountain building. Thrust faults would cause mine tunnels to end abruptly in solid rock and slow or stop mining in a seam altogether.

As the only other North American supplier of anthracite coal at the time was in Pennsylvania, the owners of the new Canmore mine were delighted. The Western Division of the CPR purchased 122,000 tons of coal from suppliers in Pennsylvania in 1891 alone and the Canmore mine owners saw a ready market. Excited about the news that anthracite coal had been discovered in the Rocky Mountains, *The London England Morning Post* enthusiastically reported on September 27, 1889, that "the monopoly formerly enjoyed by the Pennsylvania coal fields no longer exists and on the grounds of high empirical interest, it cannot be other than matter for congratulation that so valuable and so indispensable a source of smokeless fuel should have been discovered within the British Dominions of North America."

The History of Canmore

Mining

Looking across the Bow Valley from above the No. 1 Mine.

Dr. Alfred R.C. Selwyn of the Geological Survey of Canada, which had surveyed the Bow Valley between 1883 and 1885, also commented on the anthracite coal discovered in the Rocky Mountains, stating that he found coal in the Cascade Coal Basin to be "fair Anthracite, perhaps a little inferior to the best taken out of Pennsylvania."

Even if Canmore coal was of a lower grade than the coal mined in Pennsylvania, the availability of the semi-anthracite coal mined in the Bow Valley ensured that the Canadian Anthracite Coal Co. had an immediate and ready market both commercially and strategically. It seemed Pennsylvania's monopoly was about to collapse. The two-days it took to haul Canmore coal to Vancouver, British Columbia was seen as a benefit to the British Royal Navy because it allowed for quick access to a smokeless fuel; this access would give the navy a strategic advantage in wartime because the bituminous coal that had traditionally powered British warships raised a column of smoke that could be spotted over 100 kilometres away and give away a ship's position. Quick access to a smokeless coal also attracted attention south of the border, and the U.S. Bureau of Equipment tested Canmore coal as an option for American naval ships.

In 1887, within the first month of operation at the No. 1 Mine, the miners had produced 864 tons of coal, which was shipped across the Bow River by barge and then hauled to the CPR line by wagon.

The directors of the Canadian Anthracite Coal Co., buoyed by early success and outside interest in their product, had high hopes for the future of their mine and the town. They constructed extensive mine infrastructure within the narrow confines of Whiteman's Creek (Canmore Creek), including two buildings to house large fans to pump air into the mines, structures to protect compressors and boilers, and a bathhouse and lamphouse, where each miner stored his lamp when it was not in use. A tipple where the coal was sorted and loaded onto rail cars straddled the creek, and the office overlooked the entire operation.

An early logging camp in the Spray Valley.

Logging

Railway construction and coal mining required massive amounts of timber for ties and bridges, and mining companies needed lumber for underground supports and aboveground infrastructure. Every one mile of rail line required 3,000 eight-foot-long ties, and it is estimated that two feet of timber for props, used to keep tunnel roofs from collapsing, was needed for every ton of coal mined.

While constructing the railway through the Bow Valley, the CPR purchased the lumber needed for railway ties from a sawmill owned by Colonel James Walker, who was one of the original NWMP officers. By the time the rail line had been completed, Walker's operation, east of Canmore, had supplied the CPR with two million board feet of timber. In 1885, Walker moved his mill to Calgary and had logs shipped down the Bow River to Calgary from logging camps in the Spray and Kananaskis valleys. Around the same time as Walker was relocating to Calgary, the Eau Claire and Bow River Lumber Company built a mill in Calgary and began logging operations along the Kananaskis River and in the Bow Valley near Castle Mountain. Both the Eau Claire and Bow River Lumber Company and Walker's operation spent the winters cutting timber. Each spring, logs were floated down the Bow River to Calgary to be milled. Log drives continued until the 1940s. Spray Lakes Sawmills began logging in the Spray Valley, located to the south-west of Canmore, in 1954, and in 1969, the company moved its saw mill from Canmore, where lumber from the Spray Valley was milled, to Cochrane, where it continues to operate to this day.

The History of Canmore

A tipple is where the coal was sorted and loaded onto rail cars.

Mining

Word that the Bow Valley contained anthracite coal got out quickly, and prospectors and businessmen continued to view it as a place to get rich. One person whose interest was piqued was a man named Brinkerhoff, who represented a Minneapolis business group. In 1888, he hired prospectors Pat Dailey, Andrew Hamilton, and Tom McCardell to scour the south side of the Bow Valley beyond the Canadian Anthracite Coal Co. property in the hopes of finding a seam that would match the No. 1 Mine. The three men followed the No. 1 seam upstream along the Bow River to a point where they found and claimed an exposed seam of coal in a hillside that sloped down to the water.

Shortly afterwards, a group headed by Sir Thomas B. Cochrane, a British admiral, bought the Brinkerhoff claim for $50,000. The Cochrane group constructed a tipple and bunkhouse near the mine entrance, along with a handful of other buildings. Cochrane also attempted, but failed, to raise enough capital to expand the operation and build a coking plant. Out of money and unable to continue mining, Cochrane sold the mine and its infrastructure in 1890 to the Canadian North-West Coal and Lumber Syndicate. The new owners employed about 150 workers and produced 102 tons of coal each day, which enabled them to raise the capital necessary to finance the coke plant Cochrane had been unable to build.

Canmore's original economic boom was short lived. While coal mining throughout Alberta saw expansion between 1890 and 1914, the two Canmore mining companies were finding it difficult to compete against the coal mines in Lethbridge for the CPR's prairie contracts. The Galt Mines in Lethbridge had cheaper production costs as its mines were on the prairies, where the seams were much easier to mine. Even though Canmore had a higher quality product, CPR officials refused to pay a premium when the cheaper Galt coal could still be used to fire the locomotives.

In the hopes of creating new markets, the Canadian Anthracite Coal Co. turned its sights towards markets along the American west coast. Several initial shipments were sent to San Francisco, but American coal companies moved quickly to block any sales of Canmore coal in the United States and severed access to large potential markets. With the American markets blocked and the CPR's continued reliance on Galt coal, the Canadian Anthracite Coal Co. had difficulty finding reliable markets, which led to unstable production levels and in turn created employment problems for the miners.

In 1891, given the challenges the company faced marketing its coal, the Canadian Anthracite Coal Co. owners sought to sell their holdings, including the rights to 1,729 hectares of coal-bearing land. Soon after, Hobart W. McNeill, general manager of the Seattle-based Oregon Improvement Co., took control of both the Canmore and Anthracite coal mines. Although the initial plan to purchase the mines fell through when McNeill suddenly declared

Bankhead

Bankhead represents a promise made to Canmore by the CPR that was broken. When Hobart W. McNeill took over operation of the Anthracite and Canmore coal mines, his friend William Cornelius Van Horne, president of the CPR, promised not to open a coal mine that would compete against the Canadian Anthracite Coal Co. However, as production at the Anthracite mine dropped in the early 1900s and Canmore alone could not meet the railway's need, Van Horne broke his promise and, in 1903, opened a mine at the base of Cascade Mountain, along what is now the road to Lake Minnewanka.

bankruptcy, he offered to lease the Canmore collieries. The Stewarts were pleased with McNeill's second offer, as McNeill, a lawyer by training, had a proven record of managing coal mines. He had merged several American coal companies to create the Consolidated Coal Co. (he later sold this company to the Iowa Central Railroad). McNeill was also a friend of CPR president William Cornelius Van Horne. The Canadian Anthracite Coal Co. signed a ten-year contract with McNeill in the summer of 1891, with an option to extend the agreement for an additional 10 years. The contract stipulated that McNeill would pay royalties of 25 cents per ton.

H.W. McNeill Co. began mining in the Canmore Corridor in Anthracite and Canmore in 1892. That year, the royalty paid to the Canadian Anthracite Coal Co. was reduced to 20 cents

---

To house mine workers, the CPR laid out the town of Bankhead as a model community. It was attractive and well designed, complete with water and sewage systems, electricity, and 100 houses. It also had a business district that included a hotel, pool hall, school, and restaurant, as well as stores, saloons, and a boarding house for single men. A stately Catholic church was built on a hill overlooking the residential area.

Bankhead produced both the hard semi-anthracite coal, also produced at the Anthracite and Canmore mines, and the softer semi-bituminous coal, which burned hot but could not be used by locomotives or in conventional stoves. As a result, the CPR began to import coal tar from Pennsylvania to mix with its huge amounts of fine coal, in order to make briquettes in its custom-built plant. Bankhead briquettes were used to heat railway stations and passenger cars between Winnipeg and the Pacific coast.

Through the early 1900s, Bankhead miners regularly went on strike, which halted production each time. During a strike in 1922, the railway company threatened to close the Bankhead operation if the miners refused to work. Believing the threat to be idle, the union and its workers did not comply, and the CPR closed the mine. Under orders from the Dominion Parks Branch, the CPR tore down the mine buildings and moved the railway station and many of the houses to Banff. Bankhead residents moved on to Banff, Canmore, and other coal-mining towns throughout Alberta.

Today, a short walking trail winds through the Bankhead site; interpretive panels line the trail and tell the story of the town and its mine.

per ton of coal in exchange for an agreement that McNeill would operate the mine efficiently and produce a minimum of 305 tons per day and no more than 1,016 tons per day. If he broke those terms, McNeill's lease would be forfeited.

McNeill's friendship with Van Horne had an immediate effect on the viability of the Canmore mines, as it prompted the CPR to build a new bridge across the Bow River with a spur line that linked the mines on the west side of the river to the main CPR line. The steel bridge, constructed by the Toronto Bridge Co., is known today as the Engine Bridge. It is a much-loved link for hikers and cyclists on Canmore's trail system.

Hobart W. McNeill

Van Horne also supplied McNeill with a loan to assist him in developing the mine and the promise of a bonus for the coal the company extracted. Van Horne also promised that the CPR would not open a mine in the Bow Valley that would compete against the Canmore collieries.

In 1892, the year McNeill took over operation of the No. 1 Mine, he sent samples to William Whyte, the CPR Western Division general superintendent. Whyte then wrote to Van Horne to say that tests conducted on the Canmore coal had provided positive results. "It has given us such good satisfaction that I have decided to use it altogether between Gleichen and Donald," Whyte wrote. The tests indicated, Whyte added, that Canmore's semi-anthracite coal burned 15 percent more efficiently than Galt coal. Whyte also indicated, however, that he had no plans to reduce the amount of Galt coal the Western Division purchased until McNeill began mining a thicker seam, which would ensure a consistent level of production.

Charles Carey, a bold and skilled CPR locomotive engineer stationed in Canmore, modified the grates in a locomotive's firebox in the mid-1880s, which allowed it to burn the semi-anthracite coal. As a result of his work, Carey received high praise from Van Horne. A seam in the No. 1 Mine was also named after Carey. Buoyed by the positive reports from the CPR analysts and Carey's innovation, Van Horne made his famous comment: "A locomotive driver or fireman who cannot use Canmore coal will get no employment with the CPR." It was certainly a comment that would have elated the mine managers, owners, and workers.

Shortly afterwards, the CPR began exclusively using Canmore coal for its locomotives running on its line from Medicine Hat to Kamloops. The fortunes of McNeill and the Canadian Anthracite Coal Co. were finally beginning to look promising. By 1892, production in both Anthracite and Canmore had reached 25,400 tons annually. The company also purchased 1,926 hectares for $500,000, which increased their Canmore land holdings to 2832 hectares.

Although trains no longer use the Engine Bridge, it is an integral link for hikers and cyclists looking to cross the Bow River.

Meanwhile, upstream at the Cochrane Mine, the Canadian North-West Coal and Lumber Syndicate was running into financial difficulties due to the construction costs of a new coking plant and a sharp drop in production caused by severe faulting in the mine. Also, a powerful windstorm knocked over the tipple and sent it crashing into the river in 1893, which further added to the company's woes. Later that same year, the Cochrane Mine closed. H.W. McNeill Co. bought the Cochrane Mine machinery and 610 hectares of land, including two large tracts of land—Sections 20 and 21—that would later become a pivotal part of the Canadian Anthracite Coal Co.'s operations and would ensure that coal mining in Canmore would continue for many years.

Even as the Cochrane Mine and its riverside worker cottages were lost to history, the bustling village of Canmore continued to grow throughout the early 1890s. It expanded on both sides of the Bow River in what were two distinct communities, Townside (now downtown Canmore), between the railway station and the river, and Mineside, on the west bank. In 1892, a log bridge built across the river replaced a small cable ferry that transported people from one side to the other.

Construction of nearly all of the town's remaining heritage buildings occurred during this boom. In Townside, the Canmore Hotel was built in 1890, followed by the Ralph Connor Memorial United Church in 1891, and in 1893, St. Michael's Anglican Church and the North West Mounted Police Barracks. It appears another hotel, known as the Waverly, may have been built during this time as well, but details regarding this property are limited. During this time, Canmore became one of the first towns in Canada to have a subsidized medical program; miners donated $1 each payday to cover wages for a doctor and nurse, who staffed a small, four-bedroom hospital located across from the school. Other early business in Townside's Main Street area included a bakery, laundromat, pool hall, grocery store, jeweller, and second-hand store.

Across the river in Mineside, the Oskaloosa Hotel, a boarding house named after Oskaloosa, Iowa, the home town of Canadian

Mineside, with what is now downtown Canmore across the Bow River in the right half of the image.

Anthracite Coal Co. director S.E. Little, and the Canadian Anthracite Coal Co.'s store, the Rundle Mountain Trading Co., operated by the E.L. Little Co., were built side by side in 1893 just west of the intersection of today's Three Sisters Drive and Rundle Drive. The Canmore Opera House was also in Mineside. The opera house, which was built in 1898, was originally called The Band Hall and was built from logs cut down on the slopes of Ha Ling Peak. The opera house was a place where members of H.W. McNeill Co.'s Brass Band could practice. Music was an integral part of Canmore's social life, and the town was home to many fine musicians and a number of brass bands over the years, including the Elks Band. Local musicians were also a part of every Canmore parade and function.

The last decade of the 1800s was a promising time in Canmore. The village was busy with mining, logging, and the railway. It appears that everyone who had come to call Canmore home had work. An Alberta census taken in 1891 shows that children were, for the most part, the only people who were unemployed. The census also shows that men worked as coal and rock miners, labourers, waiters, cooks, telegram operators, plumbers, firemen,

H.W. McNeill Co.'s Brass Band

artists, switchmen, farmers, agents, boilermakers, storekeepers, track builders, carpenters, carriage builders, locomotive engineers and crew members, bricklayers, and hotelkeepers. One man, S.C. Diek, aged 34, indicated that he was an artist. Most of the women in Canmore remained at home; only a few women, such as Hester M. Birney, a 34-year-old, Irish-born cook, indicated that they had a job.

The 1891 census reports that the majority of Canmore's 74 houses were shared residences and were home to extended families or lodgers. For example, Birney, the female cook, shared her house with her two sons (whose names were not recorded in the census) and her two brothers, Henry and Richard, and rented rooms to two boarders, farm-worker brothers Thomas and Henrie Lusk.

Early Canmore was a melting pot of nationalities, mostly from northern Europe. The majority hailed from the British Empire, including Wales, East India, Australia, and all of Canada's provinces. Other countries represented on the census included the United States, Belgium, Holland, Germany, Sweden, France, and Denmark.

Mining

In the very earliest days of Canmore's mining history, the Chinese made up one of the largest segments of the population. Many Chinese workers had been employed by the CPR during railway construction. Chinese workers employed at the No. 1 Mine were given the worst jobs both above and below the surface. Mine operator Hobart McNeill reported in a letter written in 1898 to the deputy commissioner of the Public Works Department that he stationed a small number of the Chinese workers underground at the bottom of the slope where the trips, trains of mine cars, were hauled to the surface as "it was the most dangerous place in the mine ... They have no chance whatever

Canmore Hotel

The Canmore Hotel, which opened in 1890, is Alberta's oldest operating hotel and one of the town's oldest remaining buildings. Known by locals today as the "Canmore Hilton" or simply "the Ho," this simple, two-storey wooden building has been the centre of social life in Canmore for over 120 years. In its early years, it was the place where railway workers and miners spent their hard-earned wages; today, it attracts a wide-cross section of locals and visitors, who can order a drink at the original wooden bar and then find a spot on the veranda and watch the world of Canmore go by.

One of the most interesting people associated with the Canmore Hotel is Mary Rodda, whose family moved to Canmore from Bankhead in 1922. Six years later, she married Alfonso Rodda, a former miner who accepted a job as manager of the Canmore Hotel. When Alfonso passed away in 1952, Mary was left to run the bar, and she ran it for the next 16 years. At four feet, nine inches tall, Mary may not have been an imposing figure, but she had a presence that demanded respect from both quarrelsome miners and government officials. Even though hotel inspectors were not pleased that a woman was managing the bar, they did eventually grant her a liquor license, which made her one of the first women in Alberta allowed to run a bar.

to hurt anybody but themselves." The Chinese lived a short distance from the mine in a large bunkhouse that housed around 100 workers. Each bunkhouse provided small, semi-private cubicles. In later years, Chinese workers were relocated to two simple two-storey bunkhouses downstream from the mine buildings at a bend in Whiteman's Creek.

Records show that in 1920, the Canmore mines employed 50 Chinese workers, who were all registered by number. Pages within a mine register, under the heading "Chinamen," list each man's name, occupation, age, former residence, date of employment, and signature. Nineteen-year-old Lee Chong, for example, listed his former residence as China. Chong worked on the picking table, sorting rock and other debris from the coal. He began working in Canmore on September 15, 1909 and was listed as "Chinaman No. 39."

McNeill, adhering to the ignorance of the times, saw the Chinese workers more like children than men. He also appears to have had some respect for them, though. In a later letter to the Public Works Department, McNeill wrote that he had "tried every

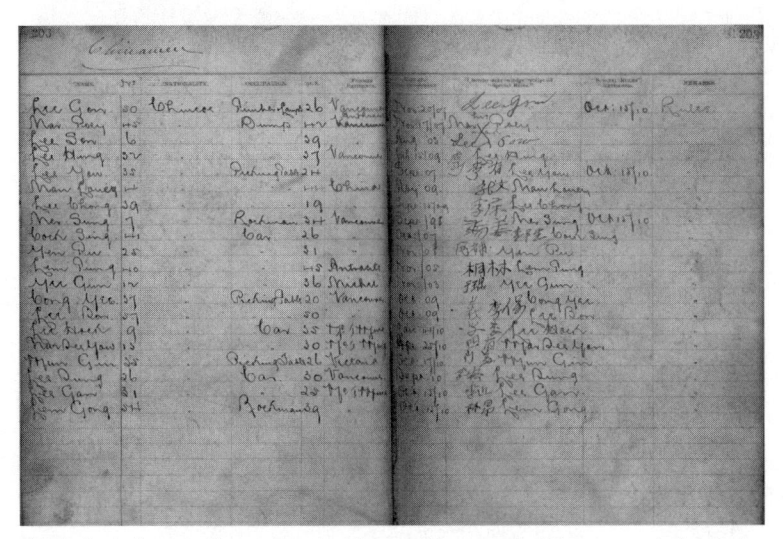

This ledger allows a glimpse into the history of Canmore's Chinese population during the town's mining era.

Mining

This humble main street store evolved into Marra's Grocery, which was one of Canmore's busiest stores until its closure in 2005.

form of labour there and they [Chinese workers] are by odds the best besides being the cheapest. Candor compels me to say they would be the best at any price." Based on McNeill's comment, it's likely that the Chinese mine workers adhered to the same ethics that they demonstrated while working for the railway.

According to Canadian historian Pierre Berton, author of *The Last Spike*, the Chinese employed by the CPR were hardworking, reliable, and honest employees who would work all day at physically demanding jobs, prepare their own meals, and then in the morning pack up and move their own equipment. The Caucasian railway workers, in comparison, expected room and board on top of their wages and were afforded the luxury of not having to pack their camps or move their equipment.

A number of the Chinese workers who came to call Canmore home later opened business such as restaurants, laundromats, and grocery stores. The best-known Chinese business in Canmore was C.T. Sing & Co., which later became Marra's Grocery. The

Chinese businessmen and mine workers often gave out small gifts at Christmas to people they knew, such as firecrackers, chestnuts, ginger, or lychee nuts.

In the 1890s, most of the residents in Canmore could read and write. Early Canmore was a typical frontier town; many liquor-fuelled fights arose among the coal miners, railway workers, loggers, farmers, and transients. Given their coarse nature, Canmore men did not impress Jessie Margaret Henderson, who taught in Canmore and shared a house with another teacher and a secretary. Henderson remained in Canmore for only a few years during the early-1900s before moving on to northern Alberta. In an attempt to draw her two friends north to join her, she wrote them a letter

A Dangerous Occupation

Although the Cascade Coal Basin produced some of Canada's highest-quality coal, it was extremely dangerous to mine due to high levels of explosive methane gas, steep coal seams that could not be mined with mechanical equipment, and seams that were extensively disturbed by folds and faults. Miners risked dealing with cave-ins, explosions, and outbursts, along with a myriad of other ways to be injured or killed.

Outbursts are sudden blowouts of methane gas and coal from a working face deep in the mine. Because coal mining relieves the pressure on a face, methane gas can be released in a sudden and violent explosion and force a massive amount of deadly gas into the mine tunnel. The quantity of methane gas emitted from the Wilson seam, for example, was over 57 cubic metres for every ton of coal produced—almost three times the amount produced in other coalfields. If a miner opened his safety lamp or attempted to light it underground with a match, a gas explosion could occur. If dry coal dust was present, it could be lifted by the force of the gas explosions and then explode, which would create a much larger explosion. And if an explosion did occur, it was always followed by a cocktail of deadly gases, known as afterdamp, created by the explosion and partial combustion of coal dust.

The largest number of deaths in the Canmore mines occurred in 1901 when an explosion in the No. 1 Mine claimed the lives of eight miners. In comparison, in Springhill, Nova Scotia, three different major coal mining disasters occurred. A fire in 1891 killed 125 miners, an explosion in 1956 killed 39 miners, and an earthquake in 1958 killed 74 miners. In Alberta, the 1914 Hillcrest mine disaster killed 189 men in a series of underground explosions.

Mining

to tell them that the boys of Spirit River were gentlemen, "unlike the mountain boys."

The majority of Canmore's men certainly would have been rough labourers, but for the most part, the violence was confined to bar fights. Serious crimes were rare, but they did occur. The village was shocked when Italian storekeeper Joseph Defeo (his last name has been recorded as Defee and Dafoe in other sources) was murdered and robbed on November 24, 1899. It was about 8:30 p.m. on a Friday when Defeo, who operated a small confectionery in a log building located one block off Main Street, turned away from the counter to retrieve an item. As soon as Defeo turned his back, the man he was serving leaned over the

---

According to former mine manager and engineer Walter Riva in his 2008 book *Survival in Paradise* the fact that only 52 miners were killed in Canmore's mines throughout its history is a testament to the skill of local workers, both miners and managers, as well as mine inspectors.

Based on the high potential for injury or death underground in coal mines, all coal towns had first aid and mine rescue teams, and for Canmore, both teams were a source of pride. Canmore had a men's first aid and mine rescue team that won provincial and national championships; in 1934, both the men's and women's first aid teams won the national championship.

Along with the risk of physical injury and death, miners were also at risk to develop a respiratory disease known as black lung, or coal-workers' pneumoconiosis. Black lung was caused by a build-up of fine coal dust in the lungs, which reduced the transfer of oxygen into the bloodstream. Over a period of time, miners would develop painful coughs, enlarged hearts, and respiratory diseases such as emphysema. Eventually, black lung, which affects coal miners today, killed many Canmore miners, especially those with 20 or more years of underground service.

counter and bludgeoned the storekeeper on the head with a blunt, heavy object. Defeo's body was discovered the next morning by a boy named William Owen, who had gone into the store to fill a grocery order. Following the autopsy, the coroner concluded that Defeo had been hit in the back of the head four times and collapsed after the first two blows. While the storekeeper was lying on the ground, the killer continued his assault. The unknown assailant stole approximately $500 from Defeo's wallet and all of the bills from the cash register. He left behind $4.30 in change. The police report stated that it was well known throughout Canmore that Defeo often carried large sums of money. The NWMP initially arrested three Canmore men—Bob Donough, Bob Nixon, and James Osborne—but released them citing a lack of evidence. "It almost seems impossible that such an act could be committed in such a small place as Canmore without some person being able to throw light on it," the report's author stated. "I cannot say that we have any clue to work on, but still we have several suspected parties in Canmore under surveillance." The writer went on to report that Canmore's Italian community was incensed and planned, if they discovered the identity of the murderer, to lynch him. Although no one was ever charged in this case, it appears Defeo's murderer may have been a Canmore man who escaped prosecution by enlisting in the Boer War.

Given that throughout the 1880s, Canmore and its neighbour to the west, Anthracite, were frontier boomtowns filled with men who had little to do but work, drink and fight, in 1888, at the request of the Canadian Anthracite Coal Co., the NWMP established a force in the Bow Valley to control drinking and what a NWMP report described as the "explosive rowdyism" of Canmore and Anthracite miners. The mine company requested that 20 police officers patrol Bow Valley mining camps. The federal government, however, only agreed to 10. When the members of the NWMP arrived in the Bow Valley, they found that the mines had been temporarily closed while the company was seeking new owners. The reinforcements were instead posted in Calgary. When the

Canmore and Anthracite mines reopened under the ownership of H.W. McNeill Co., two members of the NWMP were dispatched from Calgary to Canmore.

The police detachment become permanent two years later, and by 1893, the NWMP had built a small barracks near the south bank of Carey Creek, originally named after locomotive engineer Charles Carey, who had lived in a log house on the creek's north bank. Carey Creek later became known as Policeman's Creek. The barracks, which had an adjoining stable, was a small cabin built from logs that were dovetailed to fit on top of one another and then chinked with mud and straw. In a letter to Archibald Stewart dated Sept. 20, 1897, McNeill wrote that the police were a "God send," as they kept Canmore and Anthracite trouble free. "A camp of miners, of all nationalities, is not calculated to be free from broils and disturbances in any County. By its help our camps have been orderly, life and property have been safe, and both Canmore and Anthracite are pleasant places to live in, so far as law and order are concerned, as the best policed city in the Union," McNeill wrote.

Built in 1893, the NWMP Barracks is now open in summer as a tourist attraction.

The NWMP barracks was used by the police until 1928, when the detachment was moved to a larger building located in the Horseshoe (Rundle Crescent) on Mineside where a number of the mine managers and pit and fire bosses lived. Now operating as a museum, the original barracks was at first rented as a residence and then later sold to private interests.

Horses were another important element of early life in Canmore. The horses that were used to haul supplies within the underground mines were known as "pit ponies"; they were eventually replaced by small compressed-air locomotives known as dinkies. The horses spent the day underground and were brought to the stable at night. Horses were also used throughout the town to pull wagons, buggies, and sleighs hauling coal, garbage, groceries

Canmore Cemetery

In the late 1800s, the Canmore cemetery had been located on land initially owned by the Canada Northwest Land Company and later transferred to the CPR. Within a few decades, at least 190 people had been buried without permits, permission, or even proper records. And it certainly was not maintained. According to Department of the Interior letters from the early 1900s, the cemetery was in "deplorable condition." It was filled with patchy grass, half-filled graves, and at a few sites, the elements had exposed the coffins. As there was no fence, horses and cattle grazed on what little grass did grow. Nearby, an old road followed the gully up to the bench to the west of the cemetery. As the Dominion Parks Branch wanted to see the cemetery improved and operated properly, it bought the land from the CPR in 1922 for $70 and erected a fence around the original site, which was transferred to the Province of Alberta in 1930. The Department of the Interior also set aside eight cemetery lots to be used, without charge, as a burial ground for World War I veterans. Today, the white wooden fence remains in place, protecting the oldest graves of the original cemetery within the confines of Canmore's main cemetery off Palliser Trail.

and mail. The small farms located along what is now Bow Valley Trail used heavy draft horses for ploughing. Residents also rode horses recreationally and would take them up into the Spray Valley or to Dead Man's Flats.

In the 1890s, CPR locomotives were using around 75 percent of the coal produced in Canmore. The remainder was shipped throughout the prairies for domestic use. Having to rely on the CPR as the mine's primary market created an immediate problem for Canmore; having only one major customer did not allow for stable production, as work at the Canmore and Anthracite mines was at the mercy of the railway's seasonal schedule. The CPR's freight shipments were more active in the summer and fall, especially during the wheat harvest. However, with settlers flooding the West, both rail traffic and the need for coal was increasing. Between 1900 and 1913, the CPR's track mileage increased from 27.2 million kilometres to 83.5 million kilometres.

In 1895, the H.W. McNeill Co. began plans to build a coking plant, which would allow the company to have access to more than one market, but the discovery of good coking coal in Crowsnest Pass ended that plan.

Even though Canada's energy needs spurred other coal mines into prosperity throughout the 1890s, Canmore was struggling. Most importantly, McNeill could not meet the coal demands of the CPR. Production at the No. 1 Mine had reached 101,604 tons in 1893, but flooding in the Anthracite mine forced production to drop to 22,353 tons by 1899.

Dwindling production at the Anthracite mine was not the only challenge the H.W. McNeill Co. had to face. Hobart McNeill, who suffered from rheumatism, died in 1900 at the age of 52 in San Jose, California. While members of his family carried on in the local mining business, McNeill would have been disappointed to see how his hard work on behalf of the Canadian Anthracite Coal Co. directors would be regarded in the next decade.

7 A New Century

After Hobart McNeill's untimely death in 1900, his brother and business partner, Wilbur A. McNeill, continued to operate the Canmore mines on behalf of the Canadian Anthracite Coal Company. This arrangement continued until Walter McNeill, Wilbur's son, arrived in Canmore in 1905 to take over operation of the family business. Anticipating a long stay in Canmore as the mine operator, McNeill built himself a beautiful one-and-a half-storey house on 6.4 hectares of company land overlooking the Bow River. With Walter McNeill at the helm, the H.W. McNeill Co. opened the No. 2 Mine in 1907 on the flats next to the Bow River, downstream from the No. 1 Mine.

By 1910, the Canadian Anthracite Coal Co. had become increasingly dissatisfied with how the McNeill family was running their Canmore mining operation. It is unclear, however, why this was the case, especially since records show that in the last year that the McNeills operated the Canmore mines, the CPR had bought 270,680 tons of coal, earning earned the company $300,000 profit.

McNeill's house overlooked the Bow River. Today, the home has been restored and is privately owned.

A New Century

The view north across the Bow River around 1910.

Even so, Frederick E. Weyerhaeuser, a director of the Canadian Anthracite Coal Co. who would go on to become one of North America's best known lumber magnates, concocted a plan to oust the H.W. McNeill Co. and pass control of the mines to two of his Yale college friends, engineers Samuel Brinkerhoff Thorne and James B. Neale. The mine directors supported Weyerhaeuser, with the exception of Archibald Stewart, who pushed the board to form a subsidiary company owned wholly by the directors. Stewart wrote "McNeill was and had been pressing right along for a renewal which I opposed, I representing to our directors that McNeill had not grown with the country. I proposed that we should form a subsidiary operating company under the name of the Canmore Coal Co., with the Canadian Anthracite Coal Co. holding all the stock in it except a few shares necessary to qualify directors, and I had had the foresight long previously to secure in the department of secretary of state, the right to use of the word Canmore."

The other members of the board also wanted Walter McNeill out, but unlike Stewart, they did not see the value of establishing a subsidiary. Weyerhaeuser invited Walter McNeill, who believed his contract would be renewed, to St. Paul, Minnesota, to meet

The History of Canmore

Rundle Mountain Trading Co.

with the board. When McNeill arrived, Weyerhaeuser bluntly informed him that the lease would not be renewed; it was a decision that had been made back in Canmore while the directors toured the holdings and took advantage of McNeill's hospitality, but it had been decided that McNeill should be told at the Canadian Anthracite Coal Co. headquarters in St. Paul. McNeill, who had just lost the contract that allowed him to operate the Canmore coal mines, was also forced to move out of his house, as it had been built on company land. The house was offered to the newly appointed mine manager Robert M. Young.

As the H.W. McNeill Co. was no longer associated with Canmore, the board offered the contract for operating the Canmore mines and the company store to Thorne and Neale, who formed the Canmore Coal Co. on May 31, 1911. The Canadian Anthracite Coal Co. loaned Thorne and Neale the money that they needed to purchase stock in the Canmore Coal Co. but kept 51 percent of the shares in both the Canmore Coal Co. and the general store, which was formerly operated by E.L. Little Co. and renamed the Rundle Mountain Trading Company. Thorne and Neale received 49 percent of the shares in both the mines and the store. The Canmore Coal Co. was required to pay the Canadian Anthracite Coal Co. a royalty of 20 cents per ton, much to Stewart's disgust and frustration. "Money in the Canadian Anthracite Company treasury which could have gone to pay a dividend to shareholders was loaned to Thorne and Neale to purchase their stock in the Canmore Coal Co., Stewart lamented. "The agreement was nothing other than a 'heads I win, tails you lose' proposition. In simple words, Thorne and Neale came to the Canmore property as paupers. However, they knew their poverty would not last for long. As guests at McNeill's house they had pumped Walter McNeill and he had foolishly told them of the profits his company was making," Stewart wrote.

In the years between 1911 and 1926, Thorne and Neale personally received $361,375 in dividends from the mines alone, not including what they made from the company store. In 1926, they received a $531,594 settlement from the Canadian Anthracite Coal Company. The company planned to buy the two men out and establish a subsidiary company, which was exactly what Archibald Stewart had originally wanted. Stockholders, meanwhile, received $874,038 in dividends during the Neale and Thorne period.

Throughout their tenure, Thorne and Neale had a stake in the community and the fortunes of the mine. At the end of every working day, the mine managers sent Thorne and Neale a progress report by way of telegram. They both took an interest in Canmore, and according to Edna Appleby in *Canmore: A Story of an Era*, "[they] gave generously to support worthwhile community efforts." The Memorial Hall built in 1921 is one example of Thorne and Neale's generosity. They also got to know the miners and managers by personally visiting the mines. Stewart, however, remained disgusted by the arrangement.

Coal production throughout Alberta had jumped from 244,420 tons in the late 1890s to 4,040,000 tons by 1913. Natural gas had begun to compete against coal in 1912, with Calgary turning to gas for domestic use, but Canmore was prospering in the industry due to the fact that coal continued to be the primary source of energy for heating and transportation until 1914. Canmore not only remained the sole source of semi-anthracite coal in Canada, but was also a source of bituminous coal–a softer grade of coal suitable for coking and briquettes.

By 1914, coal mining was one of Alberta's primary industries. That year, coal mining in Alberta comprised nearly 30 percent of Canada's total coal production; 3.56 million tons of coal were produced and 8,000 people were employed.

The declaration World War I on Aug. 14, 1914, had an immediate and powerful effect on economies around the world, including Canmore's. Many men from Canmore, most of whom had direct connections to Great Britain, enlisted to fight. During the five years of war, out of a total population of 1,500 people, 97 men enlisted to fight overseas, and 14 of these men were killed. Local men Stewart Lynch and Gid Broderick received the Military

Medal, which is presented for bravery. Alberta coal mines, meanwhile, saw a substantial jump in production from 1.73 million tons in 1911 to 4.64 million tons by 1916, due to the war. Throughout the war period, miners in Canmore produced an average of 1,118 tons of coal daily; the record was 1,524 tons in a single day. The bulk of the wartime coal went to the CPR, flourmills, and farmers across Canada. Coal mines in Edmonton, Lethbridge, and the Crowsnest Pass also saw increased production, and new Alberta coal mines were opened in Coal Branch, Brazeau, Entwistle, Tofield, Camrose, and Drumheller.

Dead Man's Flats

The small community of Dead Man's Flats, east of Canmore, was named for an unsavoury incident that occurred over a century ago. Before dawn on the morning of May 11, 1904, François Marret climbed the stairs in the small home he shared with his brother, Jean, a part-time Canmore coal miner and dairy farmer who had established a dairy on the flats east of Canmore in 1901, and beat him to death with the back of an axe. Marret dragged Jean's body from the house and down to the Bow River. Shortly afterwards, Marret made his way to Canmore where he admitted to the crime at the Oskaloosa Hotel and was subsequently arrested.

At the coroner's inquest, François Marret told the jury he was the spirit of good and he killed his brother because Jean embodied the spirit of evil. "I put him in the river as I thought his ghost would not come for me," Marret said. Doctors testifying at the inquiry stated Marret was delusional and suffered from hallucinations. Despite this claim, Marret's interpreter, Mr. Winter, described him as having a gentle disposition. At his criminal trial, the jury found Marret not guilty by reason of insanity. He was subsequently committed to an asylum in Manitoba and remained there until his death.

The story of François and Jean Marret is not the only one that is said to have given Dead Man's Flats its name, however. According to Stoney artist Roland Rollinmud, his grandfather Issac had been trapping beavers when he noticed a park warden upstream. As the area was part of Rocky Mountains National Park at the time, it was illegal to hunt game within its boundaries. Issac smeared beaver blood on himself and pretended to be dead. The warden fell for the ruse and before checking to see if he was in fact dead, he raced back towards Canmore for help. As soon as he was gone, Issac collected his beavers and headed east towards Morley and home.

Prohibition

Although laws controlling the sale of liquor had been in place in the Northwest Territories (which included what is now Alberta) since 1875, prohibition officially began on July 1, 1916, to the delight of the temperance movement and the disgust of Canmore miners, who found a release in a few glasses of beer at the end of the day.

While prohibition provided police with a tool to help keep the peace, it quickly became apparent that the new anti-drinking laws would not stop Bow Valley residents from obtaining alcohol, as it was smuggled into the valley or brewed in backyard stills. In 1918, the NWMP learned that porters on westbound trains from Calgary were delivering alcohol to enthusiastic customers in Canmore and Banff. Although illegal trading on trains was stopped, putting an end to bootlegging and home brewing proved to be impossible.

While most of the local bootleggers used shacks throughout town as impromptu bars, at least one merchant quietly sold alcohol in his store. Sam Diamond, the owner of a dry goods store, was arrested on January 30, 1920, and charged with distributing a price list for liquor. He pleaded guilty to the charge and was fined $90. Records show that the year before, on November 8, 1919, police arrested three local men—H.A. Rhodda, John Verdiso, and John Riva—for making raisin wine. Police found stone jars containing four gallons of raisin wine at Rhodda's residence, while both Riva and Verdiso were found to have 40-gallon barrels of wine at their homes. It is likely that many other residents were busy brewing alcohol from anything that would ferment, including beets, rhubarb, dandelions, potatoes, and grain.

Prohibition came to an end in 1924 after 51,000 Albertans signed a plebiscite stating they wanted alcohol to be sold legally. The Alberta Liquor Control Board began opening liquor stores, and hotels across the province could apply for a liquor license that would allow them to sell alcohol to the general public. Hotel licensing rules covered everything from cleanliness and decor to requiring that patrons be seated while they drank. No live entertainment was allowed.

Although women were at first permitted to join men at drinking establishments, the law changed in 1928 and ended that practice. As a result, one room was required for the single men, and a separate room was required for women and their escorts. The Canmore Hotel's lounge was split into two sections, and a second entrance was installed; the ladies' door was on the left side of the building. The law requiring the separation of men and women was kept in place until 1967. The end of this law came about in part due to Mary Rodda of the Canmore Hotel, who was one of the province's few female bar managers.

To meet the increased demand, the mines in Canmore required enough workers to fill both a day and night shift, followed by a repair shift that was required after every 24-hour period. As over 600,000 Canadians were serving in the armed forces, finding enough miners proved to be a challenge. To help cover the shortage of workers, the Canadian government authorized the parole of enemy aliens from internment camps across the country, including one in Banff National Park. Some of these prisoners were German and Austrian soldiers, while many others were interned simply because they were from the Austro-Hungarian Empire, such as Poles, Czechs, and Ukrainians. Although they were working and living in Canada, people from the Austro-Hungarian Empire were still deemed to be a risk to national security. Prisoners of war were allowed to work on farms, at the mines, and on railway construction as long as they reported to police regularly and maintained good behaviour.

The shortage of employees at the Canmore mines led mine manager M.B. Morrow to write a letter to Major Spence, the commanding officer of the Banff internment camp, which was located in the shadow of Castle Mountain. Morrow requested that five former Canmore coal miners held in the internment camp be released. "I wish to advise you that the Canmore Coal Co. has done its best in an effort to retain an adequate supply of miners and helps to produce a sufficient amount of coal to meet the demands made upon it, but on account of the enlistment on the one hand and the Internment on the other, we now find the various classes of labour employed in the production of coal is scarce as to make it impossible to supply the amount of coal now needed by various consumers of whom we are called upon to supply," Morrow wrote. Morrow also stated that the men would be "peaceful and industrious citizens if they were allowed to return to Canmore and re-enter the employment of the mine company." He continued, saying "[It is in] the interest of Canadian industry and the general well-being of the commonwealth that the request is being made, and it is sincerely hoped by the Canmore Coal Co. that you will sanction the release of these men."

Morrow's request was granted, and approximately 350 prisoners of war were eventually released to work for private employers in the Bow Valley. Generally, the prisoners on parole were well behaved, but according to a 1916 NWMP report, the police believed that if these men had not been investigated fully and supervised strictly, they would have likely taken action to impede the war effort. "I am of the opinion that, had these enemy aliens—the Germans especially—had an opportunity to assist their country, they would have seized it in any shape or form. (They) show real feelings when incidents publicized of Allies mishap: gestures and demeanour, while on the other hand, when the tide has of war has changed in favour of the allies they have shown the intense chagrin and disappointment," the author of the report stated. However, the author may not have known, or cared, that many of the prisoners were in fact Ukrainian or another nationality that did not support the Austro-Hungarian Empire and had no interest in impeding Canada's wartime production of coal.

The influx of the paroled internees in Canmore and the fact that the federal government appeared to have considered removing Canmore's single-resident NWMP constable, C.H. Clarke (although it is not known why), caused a great deal of consternation among the leading families of Canmore. On April 17, 1918, 56 residents of Canmore, including the mine managers, sent a telegram to the Honourable T.M. Tweedie, a Member of Parliament in Ottawa, in protest. "We the undersigned citizens of Canmore understand the government contemplates the removal of all mounted police including policeman C.H. Clarke, now at Canmore. We feel that on account of approximately seventy percent of our population being Austrian and German origin it is imperative that Canmore is continuously policed ... We most emphatically protest against the government removing policeman Clarke from Canmore."

Clarke remained in Canmore and the prisoners continued to work with no overt displays or moves against the Allied war effort other than displays of excitement or disappointment shown by some of the men when the Axis forces either won a victory or suffered defeat. Housing in Canmore was limited during the war, and many of the former prisoners were forced to share beds in the Oskaloosa Hotel; beds that were left empty in the morning as the day shift departed were quickly filled by night-shift workers.

World War I ended with the armistice of November 11, 1918, which quickly shifted the Canmore coal industry from feast to

Generating Electricity

Hydroelectric power generation began in the Canmore Corridor in 1911 with the Horseshoe Dam, which was built to provide electricity to Calgary and the Exshaw cement plant. Calgary Power (now TransAlta) continued to add to its Bow River infrastructure by building the Kananaskis plant, which was completed in 1913. The next project would change the Spray Valley, west of Canmore, forever. It was a place that Father Pierre Jean De Smet described in 1845 as "a rich valley, agreeably diversified by enamelled meads, magnificent forests, and lakes."

Calgary Power first considered the Spray Valley and its two small lakes for a power-generating project in 1924. The company proposed building a dam at the north end of Spray Lakes and flooding the valley up to Wind Mountain (now known as Mount Lougheed). Calgary Power then planned to build a conduit that would carry the water to the Bow River at Dead Man's Flats by way of Wind Valley and under Wind Ridge. The plan sat idle for several years, but in 1948, Calgary Power reconsidered it as a possible way to meet a growing demand for electricity. After meeting with Canmore Mines Ltd., Calgary Power changed its plans. Instead of digging a tunnel under Wind Ridge, the company decided to build a second dam at the mouth of Whiteman's Gap. The water would be brought through by way of a canal and a penstock into a man-made lake (now Rundle Forebay) located above Canmore and would then flow down to the Bow River to a power plant adjacent to the mine manager's house.

As Calgary Power required mine land for its transmission lines and infrastructure, the company agreed to pay Canmore Mines Ltd. $200,000 as compensation. Canmore Mines Ltd. later used that money to create a pension fund for non-union workers. Work on the Spray Valley system, including an access road from the Bow Valley to Whiteman's Gap, began in 1949 and was completed by 1951. The Canyon and Three Sisters dams flooded the two small lakes, which created a 65-metre-deep reservoir with an area of nearly 20 square kilometres.

famine. With the war over, the need for coal dropped dramatically and the industry was thrust into a period of weak markets and worker unrest. And even though the miners had enjoyed increased wages during the war, the cost of living had climbed, which meant they were no better off financially than before the war. Warren Caragata wrote in *Alberta Labour: A Heritage Untold* that inflation during the war pushed prices up 72 percent. The news that the war had ended was still well received, however. Most of Canmore's residents gathered on the school grounds for a bonfire fed with railway ties and burned an effigy of the Kaiser. The residents then proceeded to Union Hall armed with food and drink and ready to celebrate; however, there was an outbreak of influenza at the time, and a law was in place that forbade large gatherings during the epidemic, so police turned the revellers away. Undaunted, the revellers filled nearby homes and carried on throughout the night.

The worldwide influenza epidemic of 1918 began near the end of World War I and eventually found its way into the Bow Valley. It spread quickly throughout Canmore, leaving no family untouched. The lucky families only had one or two members fall ill, while in some households, every member became sick.

The influenza pandemic affected many Canmore families.

Surprisingly, even though all of Canmore was affected, only one man died. During the epidemic, Canmore's medical doctor, Dr. Worthington, took over the Canmore Hotel and turned it into a temporary hospital. Public meetings were cancelled and community members were required to wear a gauze mask in public. Many locals only wore their masks when the police were around, however.

Influenza was only one of many health risks early Canmore residents faced. Another disease of note was typhoid fever, which killed at least three Canmore residents, including a young girl. William Pearce, chief inspector of surveys for the Department of the Interior, was aware of the unsanitary conditions in Canmore and halted the sale of town lots until the conditions were made better. As a result, shortly before the lease for Canmore's coal mines lease was transferred to the Canmore Coal Co., Archibald Stewart had mine manager James J. Morris install a water system to help stem the spread of typhoid. Stewart wrote that the disease had spread throughout the town as people drank contaminated water from the Bow River. "I regret to say, Canmore had received some notoriety: in other words, to be more plain, some deaths had taken place, and while it is not definitely known what the exact cause was that led to those deaths it was conceded that it was due to impure drinking water," Stewart wrote in 1913 in a letter to Commissioner of Irrigation F.H. Peters. Stewart also stated the H.W. McNeill Co. had allowed Canmore residents to collect their drinking water from the Bow River where water from the mine was being pumped into the river.

As a result of the typhoid outbreak, an aboveground town water system that drew water from Whiteman's Creek was installed. It was only workable in summer, but even so, the system reduced the prevalence of what Stewart described as "this dreaded sickness." Morris later enlarged the system by building a small concrete reservoir on Whiteman's Creek, upstream from the No. 1 Mine. He also had underground pipes installed throughout the mining camp. Stewart wrote that he had "a view of making camp more healthful for [the] people." Wells were later installed in Townside in 1924.

Even after his family's company had been ousted from operating Canmore's mines in 1911, Walter McNeill remained in Alberta. He was appointed to the Workmens Compensation Board (now the Workers' Compensation Board) and served as a member of the 1919 Royal Commission on Mining in Alberta, which had been formed after the general strike that had occurred earlier in the year. The mandate of the commission was to study all aspects of Alberta's coal industry; it was a far-reaching mandate that took McNeill throughout the province. He sought the opinions of workers, customers, and mine owners and managers in an effort to discover ways to improve the industry.

M.B. Morrow, Canmore Coal Co. general manager, spoke at the Calgary hearings in October of 1919. Even though many of the people interviewed by the commission spoke directly about dangerous conditions in their mines, problems in their towns, and even the nature and size of cots used in the bunkhouses, Morrow used his time before the board to suggest that the government

Memorial Hall was completed in 1921.

establish a board or commission to regulate the industry and improve its stability.

Frank Wheatley, a Bankhead coal miner who also operated a small family-owned coal mine in Anthracite, pushed for shorter working days and better conditions in coal mines, specifically at Bankhead. However, he referred to the Canmore wash houses as "splendid" and among the best in Alberta. Canmore's facilities were dry, clean, and warm, and miners each had a large locker that allowed them to keep their clothes dry, which Wheatley said helped to stave off rheumatism and sciatica. Each shower was separated by a partition, and as water was heated in a separate building, the miners' clothes would remain dry, unlike in Bankhead, where the steam in the washhouse ensured their clothes remained damp.

Canmore saw another community upgrade in 1921 when the Canmore Coal Co. constructed Memorial Hall, a large, three-and-a-half storey building on the site of the Oskaloosa Hotel, next to the Rundle Mountain Trading Co. Although the hall was designed primarily for Canmore war veterans, it was also used to attract workers to the community. The Y, as it was known, opened on January 14, 1921. For the most part, Memorial Hall served as a community centre. It offered a billiard room and gymnasium, as well as small bedrooms for single miners, showers, a dining hall and a reading room. Veterans were provided with a meeting space in a lavish hall set aside for their exclusive use. A cenotaph was later erected outside the front steps of Memorial Hall, paid for by the citizens of Canmore. The monument depicts a Canadian soldier and includes a list of the names of local soldiers killed during World War I. The monument now sits inside the Three Sisters Royal Canadian Legion. Memorial Hall was torn down in 1965.

The Band Hall was converted into a movie theatre in 1915, when Mineside was wired for electricity and after an addition was added to the back of the building in 1922, the name of the building was changed to the Opera House; making it was the world's only log opera house. Although the Great Depression forced the Opera House to close its doors in 1932, the popular facility reopened for a short time in 1940 and featured a show on Wednesday evenings and three shows each Saturday.

Canmore's first major mine, the No. 1 Mine, closed as planned in 1916. Almost a decade earlier, in 1907, the No. 2 Mine had begun operation along the south bank of the Bow River, a short distance downstream from the No. 1 Mine. The No. 2 Mine would prove to be Canmore's largest and longest-operating mine. It was active until the 1940s. The highest seam in the No. 1 Mine—the Carey Seam—became the lowest seam mined at the No. 2 Mine. The newer mine had its own infrastructure squashed into a narrow strip of land between the river and the steep hillside, including the tipple, the lamphouse, a machine shop, a stable for horses, and the bath, power, and boiler houses. Along with the stables and the other mine infrastructure, the No. 2 Mine also featured a briquette plant, built in 1925, where fine coal was heated and mixed with emulsified asphalt and compressed into small rounded blocks. The briquettes were sold to the CPR and across Canada as a heating fuel. A second unit was added to the original briquette plant in 1940.

Plans for the No. 2 Mine also included the construction of a small community adjacent to the site. This residential precinct was known as Prospect, and it was the first neighbourhood in Canmore to have electricity, which was provided by the mine company. The community was home to many people of Central European descent. Prospect comprised of two streets; two-storey duplexes lined the mine spur line on the south side, and on the north side, twelve two-storey ochre-coloured houses were paralleled by a row of smaller houses perched atop the high bank overlooking the Bow River.

By the 1890s, Finnish miners had established their own settlement on the west side of Whiteman's Creek. In addition to a number of simple homes, the area included a community hall that came to be known as Finn Hall. The Finnish families also shared a large steam sauna and charged other people in Canmore 10 cents to use it. Many of the Finnish houses, including Finn Hall, were built from logs stacked vertically.

A New Century

Finnish families in front of Finn Hall, which was constructed of vertically oriented logs.

Beyond the Finnish settlement, closer to the No. 1 Mine, there were a small number of little log houses and shacks, some of which had earthen floors. Some of these homes had stables, for cows and horses, and chicken coops. The mine managers and foremen tended to live in houses gathered along what became known as the Horseshoe (now Rundle Crescent), located just east of the Rundle Mountain Trading Co. and Memorial Hall. The skating and curling rinks were located in the Horseshoe, as well.

Prior to 1902, when the Department of the Interior became the approving authority in Canmore, growth in the town was steady but few controls were in place. That changed when Canmore came under the constant and harsh gaze of the Dominion Parks Branch. Inclusion in the national park gave the park superintendent and the Dominion Parks Branch direct control of the Canmore townsite, at least in Townside. Mineside was still privately owned land and faced fewer restrictions as a result. Many of Canmore's residents had built homes and businesses on empty Townside lots without leases or permits and did not pay the slightest regard to any building restrictions that may have existed. This approach appears to have been tolerated for at least a decade after the park boundary change. This tolerance ended in 1915, however, when two

The entrance to what is now Banff National Park was originally east of Canmore.

Rocky Mountains Park

Often overlooked in Canmore's history is the fact that for 28 years early in the early 1900s, Canmore was contained within the boundaries of a national park, much like the town of Banff is today.

In 1902, Rocky Mountains Park, now known as Banff National Park, was enlarged from 674 square kilometres to 11,396 square kilometres. The park boundary was moved beyond Canmore to the east, which meant the former railway town was now located within the famous park. After the boundary was changed, land in the Canmore Corridor could no longer be bought outright by the mining company or local residents; instead, land required for housing or expansion of the mines had to be leased. Park policies did not discourage mining, however. In fact, the growth of the mines was encouraged as a way to increase government revenue. This policy allowed the Canmore mining operation to expand and allowed for the construction of a cement plant in Exshaw in 1905. The only condition attached was that none of the new or existing industrial operations could impede public enjoyment or recreation in the park.

A New Century

Canmore residents, Nik Thachuk and Lee Pan, erected unauthorized buildings along Main Street. Thachuk and his business partner H.G. MacKinnon had built a large store without a permit on two downtown lots, while Pan had built a small shack facing Main Street. Rocky Mountains Park superintendent S.J. Clarke and Dominion Parks Branch commissioner J.B. Harkin, appear to have had enough with Canmore's disorganization and squatters.

Clarke and Harkin set out on a mission to beautify Canmore and bring order to the mayhem. Townside at this time was still quite small; it consisted of five blocks shaped into an "L" with Main Street (Eighth Street) comprising the long part of the "L" and Eighth Avenue the short part. Short roads, that are today Fifth through Seventh Avenues, branched off Eighth Avenue. Residences had been built along a rudimentary Ninth Avenue, which represented the western edge of town. Beyond that lay the spur line, which linked the mines to the CPR main line. Canmore otherwise ended at the spur line, which today is a walking path that leads from Railway Avenue to the Engine Bridge. To the north, east, and south of these borders, there was nothing but wilderness.

Wooden sidewalks were built on either side of Main Street and along Seventh Avenue. The roads were covered with cinders from the CPR locomotives and the mine. Residents also dumped the ashes from their heating and cooking fires onto the roads. Townside's easternmost building was the brick and stone Model School. Completed in 1922 at a cost of $33,000, the school was the first building in Townside with electricity, which was supplied by the mine's power plant. It replaced a four-room school, which burnt to the ground when a furnace overheated on January 11, 1921.

Clarke urged the Department of the Interior to take action against the numerous building infractions in order to "impress upon the people the importance of complying with the parks regulations. I think it is time that this sort of thing was put a stop to in Canmore; that plans and specifications should be insisted upon before buildings are erected, and that it would seem we will have to do something to drive the regulation home. I shall, therefore, be glad to hear from you as to what action should be taken, as in Thachuk's case he ignored repeated applications for the due observance of the regulation," Clarke wrote to Harkin in the spring of 1915.

The managers of the Canmore Coal Co. who lived in Townside were not exempt from Harkin's and Clarke's enthusiasm for beauty and improved sanitary conditions in Canmore. In 1923, Clarke noticed outhouses put in place for the convenience of workers converting the old hospital to small apartments. He then sent a letter to the mine managers, as the lot was leased by the mine, reminding them that outhouses were no longer allowed in Canmore and that the mine company was instead required to install chemical toilets. The chemical toilets were more hygienic than pit toilets, but eventually, the cesspools where the waste water was disposed of contaminated the water table, and open wells in Townside had to be condemned. That same year, Clarke also sought to tear down a derelict pig farm, located directly behind the Canmore Hotel. Harkin gave Clarke permission, stating that "[because] these buildings are in a bad state of repair and are objectionable in the townsite, you may have them removed. The material in them may be used by the indigents in Canmore for fuel."

In 1920, the Department of the Interior increased the minimum amount required to be spent on a house or business from $300 to $600 to ensure new structures complied with their desire for an attractive town, similar to Bankhead and Banff, which had both been constructed with some design standards in place, something Canmore had lacked. But as Canmore residents would find, the Parks Branch was willing to relax its standards when it came Canmore. The owner of a small shack built in 1919 on Seventh Street (where the Sacred Heart Catholic Church now stands) was provided with a lease for the lot; Clarke had suggested in a letter to Harkin that "the house is occupied and although he [Chief Warden Howard Sibbald] would not allow a house of this kind in Banff, I think it would be as well to issue a lease. The class of

A New Century

A century ago, the typical Canmore residence was a simple abode that provided a home for a miner and his family. Most homes from this era have been replaced by modern construction.

people building in Canmore are miners and it not being a tourist town, I do not think it would be advisable to be too particular as to the kind of buildings insisted upon."

Even though Mineside, as privately held land, did not face the same scrutiny as Townside, the area had grown into a full community in its own right. The community had developed from a single house and stable built in 1888 or 1889 by Ambrose Blaney, who used a team of horses to haul coal from the No. 1 Mine to the river. As a result, the mine company had used most of the available land and was forced to look to Townside for more employee housing.

Archibald Stewart, the mine manager, sent a proposal in 1909 to Howard Douglas, Dominion Parks Branch commissioner; he sought to lease 108 lots in Townside, in order to expand the housing available for miners. Stewart wanted to move the miners away from the mine; he wished to improve their living conditions and ensure that they were not near the mine or the water supply so that during a strike it would be more difficult for disgruntled workers to sabotage either the mine infrastructure or the mine's water supply.

The century-old Shareholders' Cabin is one of Canmore's oldest homes.

Stewart proposed leasing the lots in a block with the intent of installing water and sewage systems in the future. Canadian Anthracite Coal Co. planned to build one house per lot, at an average cost of $600 per house, with wells and cellars – at least in the areas where flooding would not be an issue. The company would also widen the streets to conform to park standards and extend Eighth Street to the Bow River.

The proposal suggested leasing the land for $2 per lot per year; he believed this was a good deal for the company and the Parks Branch. "[The lots] will never in my opinion," Stewart wrote to the Parks Branch, "be occupied other than by miners or men indirectly getting a living out of Canmore mines ... Since the divisional point was moved to Calgary, Canmore is merely a mining town, and the lots have not nearly the value they had when they were sold at that time for $50." The Department of the Interior agreed to Stewart's proposal on the condition that the lots were to be used for residential purposes only. While the Canadian Anthracite Coal Co. was not allowed to build licensed hotels, the company could construct other public facilities, such as churches and schools, with the consent of department officials. St. Michael's Anglican Church, on Seventh Street, was built in this manner. The four lots belonging to the church were provided by the Canadian Anthracite Coal Company.

Canmore as a community continued to grow on both sides of the Bow River, albeit slowly. Overlooking the river in Mineside, the Canmore Coal Co. completed an impressive log residence in 1910 as a place for the company shareholders to stay when they came to inspect their Canmore holdings.

Park officials also sought to control what businesses opened, with a mind to ensure a peaceful and orderly community in Canmore and Rocky Mountains Park. A 1914 application to build a brewery was swiftly denied. The Department of the Interior certainly forced Canmore to change by influencing its appearance and future, but the benefits of being in a national park meant federal money was available for roadwork, sidewalks, and other projects.

In 1926, Canmore's volunteer fire brigade was formed. The brigade's pride and joy was a Fairbanks-Morse fire-fighting unit that came with 450 metres of hose and all the necessary nozzles, and valves, along with a siren. At the same time, in the summer of 1926, the federal government approved 0.4 hectares of land along what is now Eleventh Street and Ninth Avenue, not far from downtown, for a nine-hole golf course.

When the park boundaries changed in 1930 to reflect policies in the new Parks Act that forbid mining and forestry within park boundaries, the Bow Valley and its coal mines were removed from the park (the act also changed the name of Rocky Mountains Park to Banff National Park). A number of Canmore residents signed a petition, hoping to convince the government to keep their town within the park boundaries or at least provide them with freehold title to their lots, as over the years they had paid more for the lots in rent than they were worth. Officials with the Department of the Interior advised the residents to take their issue to Premier John Edward Brownlee, as the land removed from the park would

Visitors admiring the Three Sisters from what is now Bow Valley Trail.

be turned over to the provincial government. However, national park officials offered to develop a plan with the provincial government that would enable leaseholders to acquire the title to their properties before the land was transferred. This allowed Canmore residents to buy their lots.

Between World War I, strikes, influenza, and a change in character and identity from a railway depot to a national park town, it was a difficult and tumultuous time for Canmore. Along with the difficulties came benefits, however. Canmore had grown from a population of about 650 in 1920 to over 950 by 1929, and with the growth and change came better services and infrastructure and a growing identity. These positive changes would be tested over the next few decades by the Great Depression.

In the years leading up to the Great Depression, coal production in Alberta reached new highs. The troubled post-World War I years were behind the industry, and coal production in the province had increased from 5.9 million tons in 1925 to 7.2 million tons by the time the Great Depression began, in 1929. In Canmore during the two years leading up to the Great Depression, miners excavated 271,000 tons of coal. With demand high and production increasing, the Canmore Coal Co. installed a new screening plant and built a briquette plant. The new infrastructure also met newly established requirements the CPR had for its locomotive fuel and also helped position the company's appeal to a broader market. It was also just prior to the onset of the Great Depression that the Canmore Coal Co. paid $30,000 for the Grainger Collieries' lease held on 1,000 acres in Wind Valley and on adjacent Wind Ridge (the site of today's Three Sisters Mountain Village). A seam in the No. 3 Mine was later known as the Grainger Seam.

Just one year later, however, the economic outlook for coal changed dramatically.

Although the CPR continued to be the single-largest market for Alberta and Canmore coal, Canada's road system was improving rapidly. As the amount of freight and number of passengers travelling by road increased, demand for local coal declined even further. Additionally, the coal industry in Alberta saw little regulation, which resulted in excessive competition, price cutting, and unfair practices.

Competition from the oil and gas industry was also having a serious effect on demand for coal. Not only was the railway using less coal to fuel its steam locomotives, the CPR had also begun using oil to fire its locomotives. Across Canada, the market for coal was also decreasing, especially in British Columbia, Saskatchewan, and Manitoba, where governments were either

Unions in Canmore

After holding several secret meetings at the base of the hoodoos in 1903, Canmore coal miners formed their first union. As the meeting place was beside the cemetery where miners who had been killed underground were buried, it was an appropriate location to begin discussing their rights. The primary issue discussed was pay and compensation; this issue would remain the primary concern of miners throughout the history of the Canmore mines and at mines throughout western Canada. Health and safety was also one the miners' main concerns.

In 1905, the fledging Canmore union joined District 18 of the United Mine Workers of America (UMWA), which was founded in 1890. The UMWA was not the first union that attempted to recruit Canmore miners. The Noble and Holy Order of the Knights of Labor, an American union which preferred arbitration, education, and co-operatives over strikes, chartered a chapter in Calgary in late 1886. This union had previously attempted to recruit Canmore miners but were not successful. The Western Federation of Miners followed the Knights into Alberta in 1897, but also had little success recruiting coal miners.

The UMWA represented Canmore miners until 1919, when the local workers became frustrated with the UMWA's insistence that their members should be joining the armed forces. Local miners saw a much more important fight—one

The Union Hall as it looked soon after opening.

encouraging the burning of locally produced coal or were buying cheaper American coal.

Recognizing the market for coal in the western provinces had decreased dramatically, the Alberta government began shipping coal to central Canada. Eastern markets, specifically the provinces of Quebec and Ontario, burned the greatest amounts of anthracite coal in Canada. In 1934 alone, these two provinces imported 2.8 million tons of anthracite coal, most of which came from the United States.

---

for increased wages and improved working conditions. This disagreement led the members of District 18 to vote to join the One Big Union (OBU), which had been founded during the 1919 Winnipeg General Strike. By 1920, the OBU had nearly 50,000 members across Canada.

However, the mining company and the federal government refused to deal with the OBU, which drove District 18 coal miners to the picket line. By the end of July 1919, with a strike ongoing, the UWMA revoked District 18's union charter. The mine owners and operators and the media, including *The Calgary Herald*, responded to what had been deemed the Red Scare by urging returning World War I veterans to use violence to end the strike. Large flags bearing the Communist symbol of the hammer and sickle even appeared during Dominion Day celebrations, carried by District 18 members.

But the resolve of the Canmore union, which was worn out by its fight with the mine company, the government, and the UWMA, began to crumble. The final and most effective tactic in the UMWA's plan to win back the striking miners was to send several multi-lingual representatives who were fluent in Eastern European languages to Canmore to argue their case. This move resonated with the many miners of Eastern European heritage who spoke little or no English and had previously been on the fringe of society given the language barrier.

Canmore miners voted to rejoin the UMWA on July 30, 1919. The UMWA reinstated District 18's charter in 1921.

The OBU, meanwhile, lost the majority of its members. By 1923, only 5,000 workers continued to hold membership. Although Canmore miners continued to support the UMWA and would strike when necessary, peace had been achieved for the time being.

The significant role of unions in Canmore continued until the last mine closed in 1979. Today, this history is represented by the blue and white Canmore Miners' Union Hall, on 7th Street. Completed by local volunteers in 1913, the building is used today as a cultural centre and hosts events such as live theatre.

The History of Canmore

A New Century

An aerial view of Canmore in the 1920s.

Even though exports to Quebec and Ontario provided a glimmer of hope for the industry, by 1930 the total production of coal in Alberta dropped to 5.9 million tons and then to 4.8 million tons by 1934. Exports of Alberta coal dropped from a peak of 155,760 tons in 1920 to just 13,958 tons in 1934. During this period of time, the number of operating coal mines in Alberta fell from nearly 400 to 276.

It was a devastating time for Canmore. The town's miners had their shifts decreased dramatically; in some cases, their weekly shifts dropped from six to three. Every evening at 7:00 p.m. and again at 6:30 a.m., workers listened anxiously for the mine's steam whistle, which was mounted on the roof of the boiler house. One long blast was good news, as it signalled the miners to go to work, while three blasts indicated that the mine would not operate that day or shift. The whistle could be heard across the river at Georgetown and as far away as Dead Man's Flats.

As a result of the irregular and infrequent work schedule, most miners and their families were living on credit at the Rundle Mountain Trading Co., and quite often, by the time they got their cheques, they would only see what they called "bicycle wheels"—two zeros on their pay slip. While the Canmore Coal Co. did provide for its employees by providing long-term store credit, at the same time, the company increased housing rental prices from $1 a room to $1.50. At that time, underground miners were only making 67 cents a ton, as they were paid for their production, not their time; they also had to buy their own tools and blasting powder. Surface workers, meanwhile, were making $4 a day. The residents of Canmore banded together in a typical small-town fashion, and those residents with means, such as the salaried staff and charitable organizations like the Imperial Order Daughters of the Empire, found ways to help the families who were struggling. They provided the poor families with milk tickets, clothing, and food hampers. At Christmas, the union, supported by the company and local businesses, gave each family a turkey and each child a present. It was a tradition that

Georgetown was once a thriving community just upstream from Canmore.

Georgetown

Although few traces remain of Georgetown, the town was once a bustling riverside community of 200 people. Located on the west side of the Bow River and north of the Cochrane Mine, Georgetown was developed by the Canmore Navigation and Coal Company in 1912, along with a mine and extensive above-ground infrastructure. Georgetown was a modern, well-planned community comprising around forty one- and two-storey homes that were supplied with electricity and running water. It also had a mine office, a bunkhouse for bachelors, a company store, a bungalow for the mine manager, and a community hall that also served as a schoolhouse.

At the mine site, a large trestle ran to the valley floor, where coal was loaded into railcars and hauled along a spur line that extended to the Cochrane Mine. Supplies bound for Georgetown were either hauled to the town in a boxcar or were shipped over the river by rail and transferred to wagons for the final leg of the journey, which took place along a rough road.

After only three years of operation, the Georgetown mine could not afford to expand its operation, and so with 161,000 tons of coal extracted, the mine closed. After the closure, many of the houses were dismantled and hauled to Mineside, where a few original Georgetown houses still stand on what is now Hospital Hill (Three Sisters Drive) and Rundle Crescent. After the Bow River froze in the winter of 1916, the company store, a store owned by the mine company where miners and their families bought groceries and supplies, the cost of which was deducted from their pay cheques, was hauled down the ice to Canmore, where it became the C.T. Sing & Co. General Store (later owned by the Marra family). Today, the site of Georgetown lies within Canmore Nordic Centre Provincial Park. It can be reached on foot or by bike from the Nordic Centre Day Lodge. Concrete foundations are all that remains.

continued into the 1970s. Even though the turkey and gift were a part of Christmas every year for mine employees, these donations would have been needed more so during the Great Depression.

To provide work and meals for single, unemployed men, the federal government opened a work camp a short distance east of Canmore along the Bow River. Men were housed in simple camps and worked on infrastructure projects, such as building roadways, in exchange for clothing, meals, and a monthly allowance of $5. The camp workers often walked or caught a ride into town on Saturday evenings to see a show at the Canmore Opera House. Once the Great Depression ended, many of these men remained in Canmore.

Canmore hit its lowest point in 1933–1934 when the mine, which was only operating a few days each month, produced just 113,792 tons of coal. The CPR, which had already reduced its orders of coal, also opened two coal mines in the Crowsnest Pass, which allowed the railway to reduce its reliance on Canmore coal even further. At the same time, the railway pushed Canmore to lower their prices.

The mine fared better than other industries, however, as it still had a few orders; Canmore's small tourist industry languished during the 1930s and finally died altogether, and according to author E.J. Hart, the ideological differences between Mineside and Townside ensured that the town remained divided and unable to tackle the issues of the day as a unified body.

The beginning of World War II increased the demand for production for all industries ended the Great Depression; Canmore, however, had fortunately already begun to recover in the late-1930s with an increase in sales of both coal and briquettes. The directors had not been idle during the 1930s, even though the mine had been. In 1938, recognizing that they had to improve the mine to increase its production and efficiency, the directors moved to consolidate the Canadian Anthracite Coal Co. and its subsidiary, the Canmore Coal Co. The company paid Samuel Thorne and James B. Neale $600,000 for their assets, and Canmore Mines

Canada Day Parade, 1925.

Ltd. was formed. After all these years, Archibald Stewart's goal of giving the directors full control of the mine was finally coming true. With Edmund Hayes at the helm, the directors moved forward with plans to open a new mine, the No. 4 Mine, which would prove to run two miles long and produce 2.03 million tons of coal.

Their timing was perfect. When Great Britain declared war on September 10, 1939, Canmore Mines Ltd. was in an excellent position to begin supplying coal for national transportation, which increased dramatically as soldiers, equipment, and resources were shipped across the country. Canmore coal was used in Canada to feed the railroads and power plants, as both worked overtime to supply transportation and power. At the outset of the war, sales of Canmore coal surged to 295,656 tons annually, with the CPR purchasing 101,600 tons. The sale of briquettes had dropped from 28,448 tons to 13,208 tons during the Great Depression, but by 1938, it had edged back up to 23,368 tons. World War II would prove to be a renaissance for Canmore coal. By 1944, Canmore's coal production had reached 346,779 tons, along with 101,600 tons of briquettes. Just as the mine moved to increase its efficiency, Hayes also ensured that Canmore would see improvements in its infrastructure. A new hospital was built near the top of what would become known as Hospital Hill. The two hospitals that previously operated in Canmore had been turned into private residences, which left the town without a medical facility. The company paid for the materials for the hospital, and the miners provided the labour. The mine also hired a doctor.

The declaration of war, which stimulated the need for Canmore's coal, also prompted 135 Canmore men and women to enlist in the Canadian Armed Forces throughout the war, even though coal miners became exempt from service when conscription was introduced in 1944 as part of the National Resources Mobilization Act. Surprisingly, a number of the Canmore-born who signed up for the military joined the navy, along with the more obvious choices of the army and the air force, during the course of the five-year conflict. The Evan Lewis family had five sons and one daughter enlist. Of the 135 soldiers, sailors and airmen that climbed aboard the trains at the Canmore station, 9 were killed, including Neil Broderick, Frederick Dewis, John Erickson, Joseph Hellis (lost at sea), John McLeod, Alec MacLaren, S.A. Thompson, Allan Young, and Joe Yanos. As they had during World War I, residents of Canmore designated as enemy aliens by the federal government, specifically people of German descent, had to report to the local police detachment. As many of Canmore's and Canada's young men were fighting overseas, and veterans of World War I had enlisted as guards at nearby prisoner-of-war camps, the mine struggled to find enough workers to meet the demands, and the miners that remained in Canmore were expected to work longer and more frequent days. The workweek was increased from five to six days, and a second shift was introduced.

Understandably, the miners became tired, frustrated, and prone to striking as a means to improve their situation. Recognizing both the need to ensure consistent coal production and the disruption miners could cause if they took to the picket line, the government passed an Order-in-Council banning strikes in the coal industry for the duration of the war. The government also locked miners to their jobs, which meant they could no longer leave to enlist in the war or accept a job in another industry. If necessary, the government could also force former miners back to work underground. In protest, over 10,000 coal miners working in District 18, which included Canmore, the rest of southern Alberta, and parts of British Columbia and Saskatchewan, immediately stopped working, and roughly 80 percent of Alberta's coal production ground to a halt. The government quickly established a Royal Commission that offered miners a wage increase, which increased their pay by $1 per day, and two weeks of paid vacation as compensation for their lost rights. Strikes still occurred, however. In 1946, following a two-week strike, Canmore Mines Ltd. increased wages by $1.40 per day and committed to putting three cents from every ton of coal sold into the Miners' Relief Fund. The six-day workweeks were scaled back to five days, as well.

As the war created an increased demand for coal, Canmore Mines Ltd. continued to find ways to increase production and efficiency; the company made plans to mechanize the mines. The company introduced equipment to move, load, and mine coal underground at a working face, extended the No. 4 Mine, and reopened and extended the Musgrove Slope, located in the Stewart Seam. The mine also sold its old, third switcher locomotive and replaced it with a used CPR locomotive that was designated as Engine No. 4. The miners, however, affectionately referred to it as The Goat. The powerhouse also saw the addition of four new boilers. Also, the briquette plant was expanded and the diamond-drilling program was restarted. A new slope was opened in the No. 5 Mine, which had first opened in 1923 and a new mine, the No. 3 (mines were not always named sequentially), was opened in the years immediately following the war in order to access new seams in the Cascade Coal Basin, which the Alberta Department of Mines and Minerals estimated in 1946 still had a total reserve of 2.24 billion tons of coal, half of which was available through mining. The department believed that an additional 335 million tons might be recoverable.

At the end of World War II, in 1945, rail traffic and coal production were reduced. By 1950, production dropped to 233,690 tons, as the CPR had lowered its annual contracted amount. The mines, however, were still viable and strong. Sales of commercial coal remained the same, but briquette sales were increasing, and Canmore Mines Ltd. continued to upgrade and modernize its operations.

The prosperity the war had brought to Canmore meant higher wages, as well as better conditions at the mine and in the home. Many families could afford to buy what were once considered luxury items, especially cars. By the end of the war, Canmore Mines Ltd. had built a total of 99 houses for its workers, which were rented out to miners for a nominal fee.

Otherwise, life did not change much. Work and family took precedence, just as they did before the war. Miners still met in the Canmore Hotel to drink beer, play cards, and swap stories, and families continued to attend one of the three churches dressed in their Sunday best. Young men and women rode horses, hiked, played sports, and gathered at Union Hall for social gatherings with music and dancing. Some of the men continued to get drunk and get into fights, and young men waited for their turn to work in the mines, just like their fathers, uncles, brothers, and cousins.

Not all aspects of Canmore remained the same, however. The war had introduced Canmore's veterans, both men and women, to opportunities beyond their mountain haven, such as university, new jobs, and certainly new places. Some of the veterans left because jobs in Canmore, as well as throughout the rest of Canada, were scarce because production levels in all sectors dropped at the end of the war and the surplus of men and women released from the military created a glut of workers.

The Goat

The locomotive known as The Goat was one of Canmore's most-familiar sights; it chugged back and forth along the spur line from the mines on the west side of the river to the main line of the CPR.

The Goat, a switcher steam locomotive (also known as a shunting boiler or yard goat), had a 0-6-0 designation, which means it had a total of six driving wheels, three on each side. The Goat was built by the CPR in 1905, and was designated as No. 1644; it was re-designated as No. 4—Canmore Mines Ltd.'s fourth switcher—when the mining company bought it from the CPR for $5,000 in 1943. It was one of approximately 15 locomotives that were used in Canmore through nearly a century of mining. The engines ranged from small compressed-air locomotives (known as dinkies or donkeys) to narrow-gauge electric locomotives that hauled coal to the tipple from the No. 3 and No. 4 mines. It appears that Canmore's Goat was not the only switcher with that nickname. A switcher used on the Chicago Great Western Railway between Sycamore, Illinois, and DeKalb, Illinois, was also known as The Goat.

After the locomotive was retired by Canmore Mines Ltd. in 1963, it was bought by Heritage Park in Calgary. After the locomotive had been fitted with a diesel engine and had undergone extensive refurbishment, it began its new life as a tourist attraction transporting passengers through the park.

8 The End of an Era

The most important event in Alberta's economic history occurred shortly after the end of World War II—the discovery of a major oil field. Natural gas had been used in Alberta since 1912, and aside from decreased coal sales of Canmore coal in Calgary, the use of natural gas had little overall effect on the Canmore mines. However, the 1947 discovery of oil and gas in Leduc, near Edmonton, followed by larger discoveries nearby at Redwater and Pembina, would prove to have a much larger effect.

Skating into History

Winter has always been a popular season for outdoor activities in Canmore. This was especially so in the town's earlier days, when social and sporting activities dominated life outside of work. During the early 1900s, ice sports were the most popular winter pastimes. Nearly everyone—men, women, and children—skated, played hockey, or curled wherever they could find a patch of ice. Canmore got its first covered ice rink, built in Mineside, in 1905. As a result, Canmore produced a number of skilled athletes who went on to play at competitive levels. Canmore's hockey teams (including the Miners, Roses, Flyers, and Eagles) consistently brought home championship trophies based on the talents of players like the Jerwa brothers, Frank, Art and Joe, who helped win the Senior Alberta Championships from 1926 through to 1928.

A number of locals went on to play hockey professionally, such as Annie Williamson, who played in Portland, Oregon. Canmore residents Percy Jackson, Ollie Reinikka, Andy Chakowski, Art Michaluk, Darcy Campbell, Leo Carbol, Joe Jerwa, Alex Kaleta, and Dan Blackburn all played in the National Hockey League. Many others locals competed in the minor leagues for teams such as the Calgary Stampeders, which no longer exists and the Trail Smoke Eaters of British Columbia, a team that continues today.

Leo Carbol, born in 1908, played for the Canmore Canadians, St. Louis Flyers, and Chicago Blackhawks

The End of an Era

The Canmore mines had not been put to the test this directly since the Canadian Anthracite Coal Co. struggled to find a niche in the mid-1880s. Even the Great Depression held the promise of an end followed by a new beginning. Oil and the rush to convert to gasoline and diesel did not bode well for Canmore, especially when the CPR began to introduce diesel-electric locomotives in 1937. The Leduc find was seen as the tipping point that could potentially lead to the

Skating has always been popular in Canmore.

Canmore also produced world-class speed skaters such as Thelma Crowe, who dominated the Alberta championships between 1936 and 1942; she was awarded 14 medals and 35 certificates. Crowe also won the Alberta senior women's 220-yard (200 metre) event in 1946.

The two indoor rinks at the Canmore Recreation Centre are named after Thelma Crowe and Alex Kaleta, both of whom have been inducted into the Alberta Sports Hall of Fame. Through the winter months, the recreation centre hosts the home games of the Canmore Eagles, who play in the Alberta Junior Hockey League (AJHL). The local franchise formed in 1995 under the name of the Bow Valley Eagles.

The two Grassi Lakes are named for Lawrence Grassi.

Lawrence Grassi

One of Canmore's best-known residents is Lawrence (Lorenzo) Grassi, whose love of the Canadian Rockies was legendary. Born in Falmenta, Italy, in 1890, Grassi immigrated to Canada in 1912. His first employment in his new country was with the CPR as a section hand. He eventually made his way to Canmore and began working as a coal miner. After two years in Canmore, Grassi had saved enough money to buy a small house on land leased from the Canmore Coal Co. along what is now Three Sisters Drive. Known for his great strength, Grassi was a hard and diligent worker, but when he had time off—during work stoppages and frequent periods of slow production—he explored the surrounding mountains. In 1924, Grassi built a trail to Twin Lakes, which were renamed in his honour in 1938. The trail remains an enduring and much loved legacy to this day, complete with a stone staircase and wooden benches. After officially retiring, Grassi built trails in the Lake O'Hara region while working as a seasonal assistant park warden. When he wasn't building trails, he climbed mountains (often in his mining boots), including the first solo ascent of Mountain Assiniboine. Grassi passed away in 1980 at the age of 90. Today, he has a mountain, a Canmore school, and an Alpine Club of Canada hut named for him.

decline of the use of coal and to Canmore's eventual demise as coal mining town. In 1947, Canada only produced 8 percent of the oil the country consumed. In Alberta by 1951, there were 737 oil wells and total production – if the markets were available – was at 170,000 barrels a day. As a result, 30 percent of the oil consumed in Canada was produced in Canada, which translated into $25 million a year for the Alberta government in royalties and licensing fees. Sixteen new fields had been discovered by 1953; the Pembina field, as one of the largest oil fields in Alberta, was the most important. The oil boom was good for Alberta. Numerous workers were attracted to the area, and Alberta became the prairie province with the highest population. However, what was good for Alberta at that time was not necessarily good for Canmore.

Canmore Mines Ltd. president Edmund Hayes understood implicitly that the oil boom meant the CPR's use of coal would sharply and suddenly decrease. The railway began switching to diesel locomotives and built its last new steam locomotive in 1949 (which remained in service until 1960). It even stopped ordering briquettes for heating. Even so, Hayes believed in Canmore and the quality of its coal. He believed Canmore's coal could survive the transition to oil as the world's primary energy source and that it was worthwhile to forge ahead and continue work to open the No. 3 Mine, which began producing coal by 1947–48.

By 1950, the mine was earning more than $250,000 a year, mostly from its sales of locomotive fuel and briquettes for the railway and for homes across western Canada; this profitability did not last, however. Profits began to plunge by 1953, and Hayes prediction regarding the CPR reducing its contracts with Canmore came true. Canmore saw a 25 percent decrease in sales. The winter that year was also warm; subsequently the mines only earned $90,000—bad news for shareholders and miners alike.

The following year, the Canmore Mines Ltd. reported a loss of $895. However, as Philip Hayes explained in his 1998 book *Boxing the Compass: The Life and Times of Edmund Hayes*, the loss was in the books only; the mines had written off large capital projects, including a $25,000 overhaul of the mine locomotive, The Goat. Also, both the tipple and the briquette plant had been rebuilt to reduce the mine's insurance rates. It also helped that the mine had switched to electricity, reduced the workweek to four days, and spent $500,000 to improve production and develop markets. Hayes stated that without all of this work, the Canmore mines would have been shut down—a reality other coal mining towns were facing as coal production throughout Alberta decreased. By 1959, the total output of coal in Alberta was 745,000 tons, 200,000 of which came from Canmore. By 1960, coal use across Canada had dropped 20 percent.

It became obvious that in order for the Canmore mine to stay in business, new markets for its coal had to be found. By the 1950s, most North American coal was converted to coke for use in the steel industry. Unfortunately for Canmore, though, the local coal was too soft, and as a result, it did not have the sufficient heat value necessary to be converted to the quality of coke required by the Canadian steel industry. It was sufficient, however, for a Californian company, Pacific States Steel, to use to smelt scrap steel. This resulted in the export of around 40,641 tons of coal annually, but it was not enough. The mine reduced operation from six days a week during World War II, to five, then four, and finally, by 1955, the mine operated only two or three days a week. The mining company forecast that in a few years time, total annual production would drop to only 203,209 tons.

A few factors ensured that the Canmore mine remained open. With the inventiveness of mine managers and a skilled work force, combined with assistance from the federal government and the luck of having the right product, Canmore was poised to take advantage of a new market: Japan. After learning that the Japanese steel and chemical industries were in need of anthracite coal, Canmore shipped a small sample of its coal to an intermediary, Toyo Menka (now Tomen Corporation), which in turn supplied it to Japanese industrial plants. After that first sample, increasingly

The End of an Era

The coke plant was nicknamed "Sputnik" for its resemblance to the Soviet satellite.

The History of Canmore

The tipple, as it looked shortly before Canmore's last mine closed in 1979.

The End of an Era

larger samples were sent. These shipments of samples eventually led to an order of 4,064 tons, which were shipped to Japan on May 15, 1957. Toyo Menka then placed an order for 40,641 tons. Throughout the late 1950s and into the 1960s, Japanese markets remained the key element in Canmore's ongoing success and in keeping its 225 miners working.

In the 1960s, the population of Canmore began to diversify, finding other avenues of employment; residents began working in Banff and at the Exshaw cement plant and the Kananaskis lime plant. Luckily, the local economy no longer relied entirely on coal. As predicted, the market for locomotive fuel all but vanished, essentially ending a 77-year-old connection with the CPR. Coal production during the 1960s began to climb as new markets in the U.S. were accessed through Canmore's newest product, coke. Even though Canmore Mines Ltd. had been unable to produce coke directly from its coal, Canmore-born mine engineer Walter Riva (who authored *Survival in Paradise: A Century of Coal Mining in the Bow Valley*), solved the problem in 1962 when he developed a high-temperature plant, nicknamed Sputnik (after the Soviet satellite), that could convert briquettes into coke.

To achieve the coal production required by the Japanese contracts, Canmore Mines Ltd. opened the Wilson Mine in 1960 on a gentle slope near what is now the junction of the Three Sisters Parkway and the Trans-Canada Highway. The mine was named for Canmore Mines Ltd. former executive vice-president and general manager William Wilson, who was instrumental in securing the Japanese market for the company. In 1969, the lucrative Japanese markets negotiated a $50 million deal with the company that required the production of 508,000 tons annually. As Canmore was only producing 304,814 tons by 1967–68, miners and management had some work ahead of them; a new mine was needed. Coal reserves of an estimated 27.4 million tons were available in Wind Valley, but until a source could be verified and a new slope opened, surface quarries were the answer, at least for the short term.

By 1968, Canmore's two main strip mines accounted for 63,600 tons of coal excavated annually, and they would go on to produce 355,616 tons over 7 years. The open pits were an eyesore, but the areas where they were previously located are now reclaimed and are favourite recreational spots for Canmore locals. The pits were located at what is now Quarry Lake, which for many years was simply known as the Strip Mine, and in a large meadow that has been incorporated into the Canmore Nordic Centre trail system.

Exploration work in Wind Valley, east of the No. 3 Mine and south of Dead Man's Flats, was not promising, even though the area had ample reserves of coal. More thorough testing was required, the company coffers were dry, and the shareholders

Rising Water

Given its low-lying location on the Bow River flood plain, Canmore has always been susceptible to flooding. For residents who lived near the river during the earliest years of settlement, flooding was a fact of life. Provincial records indicate that the Bow River flooded at least 19 times between 1883 and 1967. Many of these floods inundated Canmore, specifically the Mineside area of town, with water.

The corner of 8th Avenue and 7th Street during the flood of 1924.

The End of an Era

were not willing to pay for a new mine, as the mine company did not have an adequate market. Instead, the board of directors for Canmore Mines Ltd. decided to either sell or merge the company and its holdings.

Although a number of companies expressed interest in the Canmore coal mines, only Dillingham Corporation of Honolulu came forward with an offer. Dillingham Corp. and Canmore Mines Ltd. reached an agreement in 1970 and officially signed a deal in late 1971. At the time of the agreement, the Japanese customers were seeking larger and larger amounts of coal. Canmore had reached a new production record of 355,616 tons in 1971, a new record, but it still was not enough to meet the Japanese needs.

One of the worst floods ever recorded occurred on June 25, 1974. An unusually heavy snowpack and warm spring weather caused the Bow River to flood; as well, Calgary Power had earlier been forced to release water into the Bow River from Lake Minnewanka to keep the lake from overflowing, which raised the water level in the Bow River even higher. Canmore's mayor and doctor, Alfred Miltins, declared a state of emergency. The flood's crest was predicted to be the largest the Bow River had ever experienced. The flood had already raised the water level of the Bow River 1.8 metres higher than normal for that time of year, and *The Calgary Herald* reported that the river could rise an additional 23 centimetres. Eighth Avenue, Second Street, and Mineside experienced the worst of the disaster.

Hundreds of volunteers laboured throughout the day and into the night and filled the 40,000 sandbags needed to build a three-kilometre-long dike that would keep the floodwater from spreading further into town. Children even sacrificed the sand in their sandboxes as they helped their parents fill the burlap sacks that would make the 20-kilogram sandbags. By the time the floodwaters began to recede, most of Canmore's 600 homes had been flooded.

The flood of 1974 spurred officials to build a dike that stretches along the Bow River from First Street in South Canmore to the end of Larch Avenue. As downtown Canmore was built on a flood plain, water continues to flow underground, especially in downtown and south Canmore, where many buildings do not have basements. In previous years, staff at Marra's Grocery store, for example, have had to clear goods from the crawl space each spring, as water in the ground table flows through the store's low basement.

A glut of cheap petroleum coke caused Canmore's production to drop to 152,407 tons, forcing Dillingham Corp., which had just taken on full control of the mines, to lay off workers. The 1975 Organization of the Petroleum Exporting Countries (OPEC) oil embargo pushed coal production back up to 203,209 tons and allowed coal to be sold for a high price. In theory, the embargo was an unprecedented opportunity to explore new markets and make huge profits. The reality, however, was that the high cost of oil made shipping by rail costly as well, which eliminated the potential to explore markets in eastern Canadian. Also, the demand for Canmore's semi-anthracite coal was low.

By the late 1970s, Dillingham Corp. began looking to sell its Canmore holdings. Even though the company was actively seeking a buyer, however, the company continued to open new seams, including Riverside Mine and No. 4B Seam and the Walker strip mine. Both the Riverside Mine and No. 4B were located east of the old No. 2 Mine. As neither produced enough coal to meet the Japanese contract, Dillingham reopened the No.3 Mine, which had been closed at the end 1978 when Canmore had produced only 100,588 tons of coal.

The company lost money for seven out of the nine years it owned the mine. Dillingham Corp. had no prospective buyers and faced increasing difficulties in the form of tougher environmental regulations, more difficult mining conditions, competition from Australian mines, and the Japanese push for lower prices; therefore, the company made the decision to close the Canmore mines by January 1, 1980. In the previous three-and-a-half years, Dillingham Corp. had seen losses of $3 million before taxes. Charles Gregory, general manager of the mine, said losses averaged $100,000 a month.

At the end of June 1979, word was released that Canmore's last mine was going to close, which ended rumours that had dogged the Canmore workings for the previous decade. On July 9, 1979, mine foremen attended a meeting at Union Hall where they were told the mine would close later that week. Two days later, general superintendent Victor Mrokwia posted a notice on bulletin boards at the mine that stated that miners would work their last shift from 8 a.m. to 4 p.m. on Friday, July 13, 1979 – a day that would become known as Black Friday. On that day, someone with a sardonic sense of humour wrote in chalk on a door at the mine, "Mine Closed. Happy Holidays."

9 Recent Times

For the 140 employees of Canmore Mines Ltd., comprised of 108 union miners and 32 administrative staff, Black Friday was anything but a holiday. Their employment with the company had been terminated and their livelihoods had been lost. Now Canmore, a community that had prided itself on being a coal-mining town, was forced to face the reality that it was now a former coal-mining town.

With the closing of the mine, the question lingered throughout the town: "Now what?" The miners, who had been earning as much as $10 an hour, an excellent wage at the time, were offered a severance package. The miners were given the option to refuse the package in their collective agreement. Approximately one-third of the miners chose this option, to ensure that they would be employed while the mines were being decommissioned and the property reclaimed. Once that work had been completed, however, they too had to end their connection with coal mining in the Bow Valley. With money in their pockets but uncertainty in their hearts, the miners descended on the Canmore Hotel for their last drink as Canmore coal miners.

Some of the younger men and their families moved to other coal-mining communities such as Sparwood, located in southeastern British Columbia. Many of the older miners who did not want to relocate were faced with the daunting prospect of finding local jobs. To help their former employees find work, Canmore Mines Ltd. established an employment committee that sought to match jobs skills with other local companies' needs. The cement plant at Exshaw, owned by Canada Cement Lafarge, was being expanded at the time, and as new kilns were under construction, about 30 former miners found work at the plant. Others found work at nearby Thunderstone Quarries (the world's main supplier of Rundle Rock), in Banff National Park, in Kananaskis Country, and at the local hospital and schools.

Work to reclaim the mine sites, as required by the Alberta government, began on the Monday after Black Friday. Mine entrances were closed, the tipple and the rest of infrastructure, except

Although most industrial infrastructure was decommissioned after the last mine closed, some air shafts still remain, including this one along the Three Sisters Parkway.

for the lamphouse, was demolished, and the spur line tracks were pulled up. Most of the mine machinery was sold as scrap metal or buried in a large depression known as Dry Lake (now the 10th fairway of Stewart Creek Golf Course). Some of the equipment used underground was sold to a mine in Nova Scotia. It took only two years to destroy what had taken ninety-three years to build.

The mine's closure sent shock waves through Canmore, but in no way did it mean the end for the community. The town had already developed a foundation beyond coal mining and no longer needed to rely on this industry to survive. As Dr. Alfred Miltins, the mayor of Canmore at the time, explained in *The Calgary Herald*, the mines no longer played the role in Canmore they once had; only 4.6 percent of the town's population, which had doubled by 1979, the year the mines closed, from a population of 1,535 in 1971, worked for Canmore Mines Ltd.

The first steps towards incorporation of the town were taken as early as 1961. From 1902 to 1930, Canmore was controlled by the Department of the Interior as part of Rocky Mountains

Park. Following a 1930 park boundary change that left Canmore outside of what is now Banff National Park, the provincial government took responsibility for Canmore's growth and civic politics. Eventually, incorporation was seen as a way for the residents of Canmore to take responsibility for the town's direction and as a way to provide access to provincial dollars for water and sewer systems and housing loans. When the first push towards incorporation failed in 1961, Canmore residents still had wells and septic tanks, and the majority of residents believed the change would lead to tax increases.

On January 7, 1965, the newly created Improvement District No. 8 applied to the provincial government yet again to incorporate Canmore and this time succeeded. An election was held the following month, and John (Slim) Ecklof, a local insurance agent, was elected as Canmore's first mayor. William E. Millen and Floyd Bray were elected as councillors. In October, the new council took the next step and incorporated Canmore as a town, thereby opening the door to municipal infrastructure, including pavement and concrete sidewalks on Main Street. An unpretentious town hall was built on Eighth Avenue, with space set aside for the fire department and Canmore's first library. Over the next two years, Canmore underwent a great deal of construction. A new subdivision, part of which was built over the town's first golf course, flanked the tracks of the coal mine spur line. A new high school, seniors' lodge, and industrial park were also

Canmore Mayors

John Ecklof, 1965-1967
Robert Black, 1967-1971
Dr. Alfred Miltins, 1971-1974
Leo Klotz, 1974-1977
Pat Byrne, 1977-1983
Paula Andrews, 1983-1992
Bert Dyck, 1992-1998
Ron Casey, 1998-2001
Glen Craig, 2001-2004
Ron Casey, 2004-2010

Pat Byrne

built. In 1964, the much-loved Opera House was dismantled and moved to Calgary's Heritage Park, where visitors today can glimpse a piece of Canmore's history. (The Canmore Mines Ltd. No 4 locomotive, The Goat, can also be viewed at Heritage Park). Memorial Hall, built in 1921, was demolished in 1966, along with a number of houses in the old Prospect district located along the Bow River east of Mineside.

The provincial government, meanwhile, envisioned Canmore as a service centre for the entire Bow Valley. It was hoped that visitors to Banff National Park and the 4,250-square-kilometre Kananaskis Country, established in 1977, would come to Canmore for gas, vehicle repairs, accommodations, and groceries. Canmore was growing independently of the province's vision as well, as new businesses and residents established themselves in town.

The growth was so steady that by 1975, four years before the last mine closed, Canmore was home to 145 businesses and 270 motel rooms. Because Canmore had available land, the provincial government urged that the focus on development in the surrounding areas should be shifted to the town. This was consistent with Parks Canada's goal to curtail development in Banff. By 1976, 10 percent of Banff's workforce called Canmore home.

Along with physical changes, Canmore was also undergoing a demographic change. As a mining town, Canmore had for many years been home to several diverse ethnic groups, including Italians, Finns, Poles, Czechs, Slovaks, English, Americans, Ukrainians, Welsh, Scots, Germans and Austrians, along with many others. In the 1960s and 1970s, a new group of people began to alter Canmore's blue-collar demographic. Scores of younger Canadians, many from eastern Canada, were drawn to Canmore for its mountain setting and sense of community. These so-called "hippies" with long hair and big beards were both welcomed and viewed with suspicion by the blue-collar locals. Many of the locals had been connected to Canmore for generations. The newcomers, however, put down roots and added their personal stamp to the town by creating an active arts community, opening businesses, bolstering the ranks of the trades, and establishing cultural and sporting institutions that continue to operate today, such as the amateur theatre troupe Pine Tree Players and the Canmore Folk Music Festival, both founded in 1978.

The newcomers recognized the value in Canmore's history and heritage and were often at the forefront of the movement to protect the buildings and preserve the past. Their commitment to Canmore earned them the trust and friendship of the locals, which allowed them to become fully integrated in the community. Any division remaining between the adults disappeared as the children of both groups enjoyed growing up together in the tightly knit mountain community.

The Canmore Recreation Centre, located west of downtown, was built in 1983 for the centenary celebrations. Centennial Park, opposite from downtown, beside the high school, was also officially dedicated in 1983, and the Centennial Museum Society of Canmore was officially incorporated the following year. During the centenary celebrations, society members had collected numerous photographs and artifacts from Canmore's mining past for a display. It was this effort that formed the basis of the Canmore Museum and Geoscience Centre archives.

When the valley's last coal mine closed in 1979, Banff still overshadowed Canmore on the world stage. Outsiders knew nothing of Canmore beyond "the strip," a generic row of gas stations and motels along the western end of Highway 1A. Not everyone ignored Canmore, however. A number of Calgarians had owned cabins at Harvie Heights and Lac Des Arcs since the 1950s and 1960s. In the 1970s, outsiders began buying second homes in Canmore and more people became interested in the town as a weekend retreat. *The Calgary Herald* reported that by 1981, lots that had changed hands for as little as $30 following World War II were now worth $50,000. In the same article, it was reported that single family homes in Canmore were fetching as much as $120,000, and with a population of 3,100 and $14 million in development, Canmore had a greater amount of per capita construction than Calgary. It was during this growth spurt that lots in the subdivision of Larch, Canmore's first large subdivision, located on the western side of downtown Canmore, came onto the market.

By this time, developers had realized that Canmore offered something that Banff could not: land. In the 1980s, proposals submitted to the Town of Canmore ranged from practical and

Canmore Museum and Geoscience Centre

The Canmore Museum and Geoscience Centre highlights Canmore's coal mining history and interprets the complex geology of the Canadian Rockies for visitors.

Hundreds of historical photographs and artifacts were collected for a display that was showcased during Canmore's Centennial celebrations in 1983, and with all these pieces of history, the Centennial Museum Society of Canmore was able to open the town's first museum in 1984. In the ensuing years, staff and volunteers have expanded the collection while finding new and creative ways to help residents and visitors discover the human and natural heritage of the Bow Valley. The Canmore Museum earned Recognized Museum status from the Alberta Museums Association in 2007 after proving it met the standards of a professional archival organization.

The Canmore Museum & Geoscience Centre is in the Canmore Civic Centre, one block west of downtown's main street, at 902 7th Avenue. The facility is open year-round and there is a small admission charged. Phone (403) 678-2462, or visit www.cmags.org.

The Canmore Museum and Geoscience Centre is a great place to learn about local history.

feasible, like motels, to overly ambitious, such as a proposal for a ten-story, pyramid-shaped hotel put forward by Ashk Development Corporation Ltd. Another ambitious proposal was a year-round resort and recreational community called Assiniboia. Development of the community was slated for the south end of Spray Lake. Assiniboia, put forward by Underwood McLellan and Associates Ltd, was to include 320 accommodation units, a ski resort with 14 lifts, and cross-country and snowmobile trails. This community, which the developers thought could either remain as a resort or be incorporated as a town, was to have a focus on winter activities and have facilities that could accommodate up to 10,000 people per day. The developers, who believed they could have Assiniboia up and running within a few years, also envisioned a summer component and wanted to include a golf course, marina, and campgrounds.

As far back as 1977, the Calgary Regional Planning Commission recognized that interest in the Canmore Corridor was growing and that developers, the municipality, its residents, and the surrounding Improvement Districts would need direction to manage future growth. The commission undertook a study that evaluated prospects and possibilities for the corridor. As part of the report, the commission surveyed Canmore residents to gauge how they perceived the current and proposed future use of the Corridor. The surveys demonstrated a division. Mining was the highest priority for permanent residents, while the seasonal residents believed recreation was a more appropriate use for this region. Permanent residents and the business community saw value in expanding tourism.

Both sides agreed that growth, which was inevitable, would be good for Canmore and that any development, including expansion of the valley's coal mines, which were still operating at the time, and limestone quarries, had to be well planned and have a low impact on the environment. The report also indicated a growing environmental movement and the residents' changing perception; many residents now acknowledged that tourism and recreation could potentially offer a greater financial reward than coal mining.

But even by the mid-1980s, visitors to the Canadian Rockies still had no incentive to explore Canmore beyond "the strip" and its row of gas stations and motels, including the A-1 Motel with its row of tipi-shaped units. This motel gave the residential area sandwiched between Highway 1A and the Trans-Canada Highway the nickname "Teepee Town", using the anglicized spelling.

A turning point was reached when Dillingham Corporation sold its extensive land holdings east of Canmore, where the Three Sisters Mountain Village is located today. The company had originally considered developing its Canmore property for resorts in 1972 and drew up conceptual plans illustrating a downhill ski resort and extensive summer recreational facilities, including cottages, golf courses, and artificial lakes, that would accommodate 5,000 people. The developers also envisioned a commuter train running between Canmore and Calgary. Eventually, however, the company decided that the Canmore Corridor climate was not conducive for downhill skiing and that summer development would only work if the extensive mine scars, specifically the strip mines, were rehabilitated. In 1980, the 1,200-hectare property was sold to KGM Developments, owned at that time by Calgary-resident Richard Melchin, for a reported $5 - $7 million. Melchin also bought a 60-hectare parcel of land located within the town boundaries.

The following year, Patrician Land Corp. headed by the owner of the Edmonton Oilers at the time, Peter Pocklington, bought KGM Developments. Melchin remained president of the company. The first major development planned on the property was Echo Valley, a 300-hectare subdivision in Wind Valley, comprising 3,135 residential units, a 500-room hotel, and 500 time-share units. The proposed year of completion of Echo Valley was 1988.

Instead of optimism and progress, however, the spring of 1982 brought delays and overruns, including additional servicing costs in the nearby Rundleview development, subsidence in the No. 1

Ha Ling Peak

For nearly a century, one of the most distinctive mountains visible from Canmore was known as Chinaman's Peak. The mountain was named in the 1890s without intended malice, as the implications of this name were not fully understood at the time. In 1996, a group of Chinese Canadians requested that the provincial government rescind the name.

The request immediately sparked a bitter debate that lasted for almost a year. The debate took place in letters to newspapers, on the streets and in local cafes, and at public meetings hosted by the Alberta Historical Resources Foundation Board. Both sides started petitions, and the petition that supported a name change received slightly more signatures.

On one side of the debate, it was argued that the name honoured not only the Chinese worker who had climbed the peak in 1896, but the Chinese history in Canmore. Some suggested the name was a valuable history lesson on how minorities in Canada were treated in the late 1800s. On the other side, Chinese Canadians argued that the name was a painful reminder of Canada's institutionalized racism. Calgarian Alfred Chow raised the issue in 1996 when he wrote to the Minister of Community Development. He sought to have the name removed because of what it represented to Chinese Canadians. Roger Mah Poy of Canmore shared this view, and said the name symbolized oppression, not honour. Calgarian Pearl Yip argued that although she advocated the name change, she was not trying to alter the history of Canmore as it was her history as well.

Some suggested that by renaming the mountain Ha Ling Peak, the original name would in some way be restored as an 1896 article in the *Medicine Hat News* called it Ha Ling Peak. On October 22, 1896, the *Medicine Hat News* reported that a 28-year-old railway cook named Ha Ling raced to the 2,680-metre unnamed summit from the valley floor. Ha Ling reached the peak in less than 10 hours and thereby won a $50 bet he had made with other Chinese railway workers.

Ha Ling left Canmore at 7:00 a.m. and returned, after planting a small flag at the peak's summit, about 12:30 p.m., which was four-and-a-half hours earlier than his co-workers had expected. The men he had made the bet with were dubious, however. They had been watching the summit with field glasses the entire time, but both Ha Ling and his flag were too small to be seen. "The Chinese who lost the bet, having doubts that Ha Ling ever got to the top of the peak, agreed that before paying the money several of those interested should go up with him the following day, and if the flag was found on top of the mountain, would be handed over," the article in the *Medicine Hat News* stated. The following day, Ha Ling led a few men to the summit, where they found his small flag fluttering the breeze. In agreement that Ha Ling had won the bet, the men unfurled a two-metre-wide scarlet flag mounted on a four-metre pole, which could easily be seen from town. "The flag and the flagstaff can now be seen by the naked eye. As the peak has no

Ha Ling Peak from Quarry Lake

name let it henceforth be called 'Ha Ling Peak' in honour of his daring intrepidity," the article stated.

One century after Ha Ling's climb, after much discussion, Alberta Community Development Minister Shirley McClellan announced on May 27, 1997, that the name Chinaman's Peak would be rescinded, and the process of selecting a new name commenced. There was little doubt as to what the final decision would be, and in July 1998, the Alberta Historical Resources Foundation officially changed the name of the mountain to Ha Ling Peak.

Mine workings, and the necessary purchase of an expensive water filtration system. Those problems were minor, however, compared to the issues Patrician Land Company faced in 1983 when its parent company, Fidelity Trust Co., collapsed and ultimately left Canadian taxpayers with a $359-million bill.

But in the early 1980s, as Patrician Land Corp. and its grand plan were fading from the Canmore landscape, there was much speculation and many fingers crossed in the hopes that the 1988 Olympic Winter Games would be awarded to Calgary; Canmore would serve as co-host if Calgary won the bid. Initial planning for Calgary's bid submission began in 1979. The Calgary Olympic Development Association originally sought Mount Sparrowhawk, located south of Canmore in the Spray Valley, as the site for the alpine events. Eventually, the Olympic bid committee decided upon Mount Allan (which was subsequently renamed Nakiska, a Cree word that means "to meet") in Kananaskis Country along Highway 40 as the proposed site for downhill skiing events. The venue change was a serious blow to Canmore. It was thought that the development of Mount Sparrowhawk would have provided an estimated 1,500 jobs during what was proving to be a tough recession characterized by extremely high interest rates, inflation, a high rate of unemployment, and the closure of the last Canmore mine.

Built for the 1988 Winter Olympic Games, the Canmore Nordic Centre continues to host athletes from around the world at cross-country skiing and biathlon events.

However, local spirits brightened when on September 30, 1981, Calgary was awarded the XV Olympic Winter Games over bids submitted by Falun (Sweden) and Cortina d'Ampezzo (Italy). Canmore residents also soon learned of a rumour that the cross-country skiing and biathlon events would not be held in Bragg

Mount Lougheed

Mount Lougheed

East of Canmore at Dead Man's Flats, Mount Lougheed dominates the southern skyline. This 3,105-metre-high peak was originally named Wind Mountain by Eugene Bourgeau, a botanist who first spotted it while collecting plants on the 1858 Palliser expedition. Bourgeau was unusual among early explorers; when he named natural features, he used descriptive names rather than the names of famous people.

The mountain was renamed in 1928 after Sir James Alexander Lougheed, a prominent Calgary businessman and politician. One year after the CPR completed its rail line to Calgary, Lougheed arrived in the frontier city and established a law office; the CPR was his first major client. At just 35 years old, Lougheed was appointed to the Senate as a supporter of Western interests. He was knighted in 1916 and is the only Albertan to ever receive this honour. His grandson, Peter Lougheed, was the premier of Alberta from 1971 to 1985.

The mountain's original name was revived when a peak immediately to the south was named Wind Mountain in 1985. To the west is the distinctive spire of the Windtower. The similarity of the names can be somewhat confusing for people.

Creek, as originally proposed, but instead in their hometown. The site change became official in October 1983.

A 1985 tourism development strategy suggested using the Olympics and the international exposure they would bring to promote Canmore. The report also suggested that Canmore position itself during the Olympics as a staging area for world-class recreation opportunities, advance its heritage values, and encourage its arts community, nightlife and entertainment. The report also recommended improving the local trail system and attracting a major resort development. The 1985 strategy made it clear that all of the studies and literature regarding Canmore shared a common theme: Canmore was an ideal place for a resort given its location, scenery, and potential for future development.

New residential development had already begun. Shortly before it was announced that Canmore would co-host the Olympics, the Benchlands Trail overpass opened over the Trans-Canada Highway. The highway had been built through the Bow Valley in 1962, and in the late 1960s it was upgraded to four lanes and extended to the Banff National Park east gate. The overpass linked residential and commercial lots in the newly subdivided Cougar Creek and Elk Run developments to the historic heart of Canmore. The Larch subdivision, at the western edge of Canmore, had also been completed. Homes had been built in this subdivision by the late 1970s and early 1980s.

As Canmore celebrated its centenary in 1983, work to secure the town's future was well underway. Construction on the $15.4 million Canmore Nordic Centre, designed to host the cross-country, biathlon, and Nordic combined events at the 1988 Olympic Winter Games, began in late 1984. Mostly funded by the provincial government, $6 million was spent on the 600-bed Athletes' Village alone, which comprised temporary housing beside the Canmore Recreation Centre. The municipality spent an additional $1.45 million on a legacy of the Olympic games, a new swimming pool, a curling rink, and an upgraded golf clubhouse, which were all used during the Olympics.

Finally, after years of planning, construction, and anticipation, the Olympic torch arrived at the Canmore town limits on the afternoon of February 13, 1988. The torch's arrival signalled the official start of the games for Canmore and its excited residents. It was presented to Stoney chief John Snow and a group of Stoney dancers, who in turn passed it down a line of Canmore residents standing along Highway 1A. Johnny Boychuk, Canmore's gentleman cowboy who founded Cross Zee Ranch, was the first local resident to have the honour of holding the torch. Boychuk, known for his distinctive moustache, dropped his cane and held the torch high for his allotted three seconds before passing it on to the next person in line. Boychuk, who passed away in 2006 at the age of 101, later described participation in the torch relay as one of the highlights of his life. By the time the torch reached its final destination at the Canmore Nordic Centre, it had passed through the hands of an estimated 6,000 people. The torch was scheduled to travel through places such as the Canmore Hospital and local seniors' lodge, in order to ensure that everyone was included in the once-in-a-lifetime experience. At the Nordic Centre, many hours behind schedule, Lionel Fournier, Canmore resident and former Olympic decathlete, and Thelma Crowe, the 1936 Alberta speed skating champion whose name graces one of the rinks at the Canmore Recreation Centre, used the torch to light a miner's lamp. The cauldron at the Canmore Nordic Centre was lit the following morning, just prior to the start of the first cross-country skiing event.

February 1988 had begun with the promise of a typical Canadian Rockies winter. Temperatures were well below freezing, but, as often happens in southwest Alberta, a chinook rolled in on February 10, just three days before the opening ceremonies, and high winds and warm temperatures affected all outdoor venues. On Feb. 11, the temperature in Calgary jumped from -19.5 degrees Celsius to 5.5 degrees Celsius. During the 16 days of the Olympic Winter Games, the University of Calgary weather station registered only two days where the temperature dipped below freezing.

For five days, the temperature was above 11 degrees Celsius. On February 24, the temperature reached 19.5 degrees Celsius. This was the highest temperature recorded in the month of February in 50 years.

Alpine Club of Canada

The Canmore-based Alpine Club of Canada (ACC), like similar clubs in the United States and Great Britain, is a nonprofit mountaineering organization whose objectives include encouraging mountaineering through educational programs, exploring and studying alpine and glacial regions, and preserving mountain flora and fauna.

The club was formed in 1906, mainly through the tireless campaign of its first president, Arthur Wheeler. A list of early members reads like a Who's Who of the Canadian Rockies—Lawrence Grassi, Bill Peyto, Tom Wilson, Byron Harmon, Mary Schaffer—names familiar to anyone who spends time in the region.

The original clubhouse was on the outskirts of the town of Banff, but in 1980 a new clubhouse was built on benchland at the edge of Canmore to serve as the association's national headquarters. The club's ongoing projects include operating the Canadian Alpine Centre (Lake Louise Hostel), maintaining a system of huts throughout the backcountry of the Canadian Rockies, and publishing the annual *Canadian Alpine Journal*.

Like Calgary, Canmore also experienced relatively warm weather. Competitors participating in the ice sculpting competition were forced to work quickly. Their masterpieces melted as they worked. Snow at the Canmore Nordic Centre melted during the day and froze at night, which forced repair work to be done on the course and coaches and athletes to spend much of their time trying to find the perfect wax for the rapidly changing conditions. Throughout the games, residents, athletes, and spectators enjoyed downtown Canmore in short-sleeved shirts and shorts. Bars and restaurants with patios were booming with business as people took advantage of the unexpected temperatures.

Along with the chinook came strong winds. At the top of the downhill skiing course at Nakiska, winds were clocked as high as 160 kilometres per hour. The winds also wrecked havoc at the Canmore Nordic Centre on February 21. Not one of the 71 competitors in the biathlon hit all 20 targets in the shooting portion of the men's 20-kilometre race, due to the high winds.

The weather did not dampen the Olympic experience, however, and most residents and visitors were sad to see the Olympic Winter Games and its festival-like ambience end. For business owners, the games provided an above-average level of sales for February, but overall, sales were not as high as had been anticipated. Motels were the one segment of the business community that exceeded typical February bookings.

After the closing ceremony of the 1988 Olympics, held on February 28, temporary infrastructure at the Athletes' Village and the Nordic Centre was dismantled and the Olympic facilities were opened to the public. The pool was the first public pool in Canmore. The Canmore Nordic Centre has since hosted a number of world-class winter sporting events, including the 1992 Biathlon Junior World Championships and the 2010 Alberta World Cup cross-country skiing event.

Paula Andrews, the mayor at the time, was confident that the international recognition Canmore had received during the 1988 Winter Olympic Games would increase tourism and related development, but she also believed a prominent hotel that had appeal to international visitors was necessary for future growth in the tourism sector. She may have been right; even though the Olympics brought exposure to Canmore, tourism remained slow. In 1989, Canmore saw only 200,000 visitors, while Banff had 3.2 million and the Kananaskis Country 1.6 million that same year.

Regardless of visitor numbers, due to its setting and recreational opportunities, Canmore was still seen as a place of "significant tourism potential," according to the 1990 Bow-Canmore Area Market Demand Study. Like Andrews, the writers of the study believed that in order for Canmore to become a destination in itself, the town needed facilities that were attractive to international visitors. The mountain scenery, along with the potential for residential, commercial, and recreational development, continued to be Canmore's greatest asset. However, the town had a number of challenges to overcome before it could hope to attract the high numbers of tourists its neighbours did. It was felt by those championing Canmore as a tourist destination that the town needed public transportation to local ski resorts, resort-style golfing, a convention centre, more upscale accommodations, better restaurants, and more refined shopping experiences.

All of these improvements and more were incorporated into the ambitious Three Sisters development plan, which was the latest version of what the Dillingham Corporation originally proposed in 1972. The new master plan for the property that extended east from town along the Canmore Corridor included golf courses, hotels, and a number of new neighbourhoods, such as Homesteads, Lamphouse Rise, Village Townhouses and Peaks of Grassi (at the west end of the site). In 1998, TGS Properties, the latest in a string of owners, put forward yet another master plan for Three Sisters resort. This plan included three eighteen-hole golf courses, one of which would be semi-private and have a clubhouse in Wind Valley, which is located at the base of Mount Lougheed, three-, four- and five-star hotels totalling 2,425 rooms, a community centre, and approximately 2,000 residential lots. It was estimated that the resort would add about 15,000 residents to Canmore's total population, as well as 6,085 housing units and 700 staff housing units. Throughout the resort, housing would range from single-family homes to estate homes, townhouses, apartments, modular homes and staff housing, and low- and modest-cost housing. It was also estimated that once completed, the resort

Black bears are one of the many species who use local wildlife corridors.

Wildlife Corridors

The Bow Valley is only four kilometres wide in the Canmore area, and development is extending across the valley; therefore, little room is left for wildlife. The terrain most suitable for travelling has been occupied by roads, a railway, and housing, which has made it difficult for animals to move around the area.

Following the building boom that occurred after the 1988 Olympic Winter Games, local land managers began to realize that the growing town was becoming a plug that blocked wildlife movement through the valley. Government biologists and officials approached Canmore's town council in 1992 hoping to offer a solution that would ensure that the valley's integrity as a wild space was not destroyed. The biologists suggested establishing protected wildlife movement corridors that would provide animals with a route along the valley.

Many animals travel great distances within their lifetime. Some migrate between winter and summer habitats or within large home ranges. Deer, elk, bears, would create 7,000 jobs and an increased tax assessment for the Town of Canmore of roughly $580 million.

The total amount of available land with the town of Canmore was quite small at the time of incorporation in 1965. By 1982, the town began planning to annex land outside its boundaries, but no official changes were made. In 1991, the annual population

---

cougars, wolves, coyotes, and even wolverines travel the length of the Bow Valley. Through primary corridors and the associated habitat patches, areas where animals can feed and rest, wildlife can move along either side of the valley or follow secondary corridors across it. Animals can also use the wildlife underpasses to cross the Trans-Canada Highway.

The Town of Canmore was receptive to the idea of creating wildlife corridors, but faced the challenge of creating a workable plan. Cooperating with government biologists, the town council eventually developed guidelines that restricted development in 200- to 300-metre-wide corridors.

At first, local developers were uncertain about these new requirements. Over time, however, they agreed that the restrictions would be to the long-term benefit of valley wildlife. On the north side of the Bow Valley, the Eagle Terrace and Silvertip developments were the first to incorporate corridors in their plans. Canmore-born developer Frank Kernick went a step further with his Eagle Terrace development and donated 30 hectares of its land to the Rocky Mountain Elk Foundation (RMEF) to be set aside for a secondary wildlife corridor. To further ensure the land would not be developed in the future, the RMEF and Canmore town council approached the Nature Conservancy of Canada and requested a conservation easement that, with the landowner's consent, restricted development on the land.

On the south side of the valley, wildlife corridors in Three Sisters Mountain Village were established during the Natural Resources Conservation Board (NRCB) hearings of 1992. Following the hearing, the NRCB required Three Sisters Mountain Village to establish a multi-species wildlife corridor that would connect Wind Valley, which is located on the eastern edge of the Three Sisters Mountain Village boundary, to the eastern edge of Banff National Park. The NRCB also established the Bow Corridor Ecosystem Advisory Group in 1995. The group, comprised of representatives from various municipalities and government organizations in the region, was responsible for establishing criteria for corridors between Banff National Park and Seebe.

The challenge for the future is to ensure that the corridors continue to function effectively, especially as Canmore's development footprint expands and the population increases.

growth rate was 10 percent and developable land within the town limits was scarce. In response to concerns that land would be at a premium within four to five years, the town sought to annex 6,400 hectares in five separate parcels from the MD of Bighorn and Improvement District Nos. 5 and 8. The parcels included the Three Sisters lands, the hamlets of Harvie Heights and Dead Man's Flats, a portion of land located in Kananaskis Country, and what was being referred to as the Grassi Lakes lands (near Quarry Lake). With the proposed annexation, Canmore would have a 35-year supply of land and an opportunity to solve serious social issues, including a shortage of low-cost and staff housing. Out of all these parcels, the Three Sisters lands were the most important to annex because the council at the time did not want to see a new and separate town develop on its eastern border. The councillors instead wanted those lands to be a part of Canmore's tax and economic base. By August 1991, the provincial government approved the annexation of 5,390 hectares.

Given the size of the Three Sisters proposal, the Natural Resources Conservation Board (NRCB), an independent body appointed by the province, held a special, nine-day hearing in June 1992 to determine if the development was the best use for that land. After considering the evidence presented, the board released a decision stating that Three Sisters would have "substantial beneficial economic effects" on Canmore and Alberta as a whole. The final report was not all positive; it stated that the development would increase Canmore's population quickly and create social problems. However, the board believed these problems could be managed. They also recognized that the scale of the development would have environmental effects, but again, it was thought that these issues could be managed and were not serious enough to curtail or block development. The NRCB refused to allow development to occur in the environmentally sensitive Wind Valley portion of the Three Sisters property, however.

Following the NRCB decision, the provincial government passed Section 619 of the Alberta Municipal Government Act.

Streets in the Prospect neighbourhood are named for prominent people who have contributed to Canmore's history.

This was a retroactive amendment that gave the NRCB and other government boards priority over a municipality when land-use issues relating to projects that adhered to the NRCB arose. Section 619, which became known as the "Canmore Clause," also forced municipalities to approve any development that met the criteria of NRCB decisions.

Three Sisters, as the largest development proposed for the Canmore Corridor, garnered much of the attention in the 1990s, but there were several other developments that passed the initial tests and attained funding. Construction still continues to this day at some of these developments. Silvertip, owned by Stone Creek Resorts, occupies a 250-hectare site on the north side of the valley. The first residential lots on the development came onto the market in 1993, and today, Silvertip includes a world-class 18-hole golf course surrounded by stylish alpine-inspired residences. Downtown, third-generation Canmore resident Frank Kernick has transformed what was once a dairy farm into Spring Creek Mountain Village, where housing options range from upscale condos to residences designed especially for working artists.

Other notable proposals, included an 18-hole golf course and RV Park at Dead Man's Flat proposed by BHB Canmore Resorts Ltd. After 15 years of planning with the MD of Bighorn, the proposal changed from a 110-hectare resort to a 13-hectare mixed residential and light industrial development. Kan-Can Resorts Ltd., meanwhile, proposed an expansion of the Alpine Resort Haven on Pigeon Mountain. Proposals were also put forth for an 18-hole golf course at the Kananaskis Guest Ranch, which was completed in 2009, numerous new hotels along Highway 1A, and townhouse and condominium developments surrounding the downtown core and between Highway 1A and the Trans-Canada Highway.

For most of the 1990s, Canmore's population increased by 9 to 10 percent annually; this was almost double the annual increase experienced during the previous decade. With an enormous number of proposed developments, it is not surprising that residents grew increasingly worried about their town and way of life. Many residents did not want to see Canmore expand at the expense of small-town values. Property prices were continuing to climb, which meant good news for owners but spelled frustration for young families or those without the means to purchase property. Rising property prices generated concerns regarding affordable housing, environmental issues, and a lopsided tax base that reflected the lack of commercial and retail businesses in town. But through careful planning, input from all interested parties, and a general consensus that Canmore is a wonderful place to call home, the town has overcome many of the pitfalls experienced by other boomtowns.

Today, with its desirable surroundings, fantastic recreational opportunities, and convenient location (between Calgary and Banff), Canmore's population has grown to 12,000 permanent residents. The most recent census also recorded that Canmore has an additional 5,600 non-permanent residents (people who own residences in Canmore but live elsewhere). The streets of downtown Canmore have been revitalized, demand remains strong for both commercial and residential developments, and the number of innovative restaurants and boutique shops continue to grow. A strikingly modern Canmore Civic Centre opened in downtown in 2004. The Canmore Nordic Centre hosts world-class events in both the summer and winter, and outdoor enthusiasts take full advantage of the hiking and biking trails that now lace the valley. Annual events such as the Canmore Folk Music Festival, artsPeak, and the Canmore Highland Games draws thousands of people, and the fairways of three world-class golf courses attract golfers from around the world.

Canmore's long and colourful journey from past to present is kept alive through vibrant memories and historical sites, buildings, and artifacts. The Canmore Museum and Geoscience Centre is one of the best places to begin exploring the town's history. Within walking distance of the museum, both locals and visitors can immerse themselves in Canmore's past while wandering through the NWMP barracks or enjoying a drink at the century-old Canmore Hotel. Canmore's more distant history can be discovered at Grassi Lakes and Grotto Canyon, where pictographs remind us of the valley's earliest visitors. Hikers can follow the footsteps of Ha Ling by climbing his namesake peak while the less adventuous can view mining relics closer to town or enjoy annual celebrations such as Miners' Day.

Canmore Timeline

9000 BC	Paleo-Indians first visit the Bow Valley
1650s	Stoney begin hunting in the Bow Valley
1800	David Thompson is the first European to lay eyes on the Canmore Corridor
1832	Peigan Post is established
1841	James Sinclair passes through the Canmore Corridor
1845	James Warre painting depicts local natural landmarks
1845	Father De Smet crosses Whiteman's Gap
1847	Reverend Robert Rundle preaches to local Stoney
1858	Palliser Expedition passes through the Bow Valley
1859	The Earl of Southesk is the valley's first tourist
1871	Surveying begins for a transcontinental railway
1873	McDougall family establishes a mission at Morley
1883	Transcontinental rail line reaches the Bow Valley
1884	Siding 27 is renamed Canmore
1884	Coal is discovered near Whiteman's Creek
1886	A settlement grows around the railway station

The Earl of Southesk

Canmore Timeline

1887	Canmore's first coal mine begins operation
1888	The NWMP establish a post in Canmore
1902	Canmore falls within the boundaries of an expanded Rocky Mountains Park
1914	World War I leads to increased demand for coal
1916	No. 1 Mine closes, No 2 opens
1920	Canmore's population is 650
1926	Canmore Fire Brigade is formed
1933	Coal production dips to 113,792 tons
1939	Production surges at the onset of World War II
1947	Oil and gas are discovered near Edmonton
1965	The town of Canmore is incorporated
1971	Dillingham Corp. purchases Canmore mining operations
1977	Kananaskis Country is established
1979	The last Canmore mine closes
1983	Canmore celebrates its centenary
1988	Canmore hosts Nordic events of the Winter Olympic Games
1993	First lots at Silvertip are sold
2004	Canmore Civic Centre opens
2010	Olympic Torch passes through Canmore

Canmore in the 1880s

The Canmore Civic Centre opened in 2004.

Further Reading

Appleby, Edna. *Canmore: The Story of an Era*. Canmore: self-published, 1975. *Canmore: The Story of an Era* was the first book to record Canmore's history. Although the book is now out of print, it is an invaluable reference.

Berton, Pierre. *The Last Spike: The Great Railway 1881–1885*. Toronto: McClelland and Stewart Ltd., 1971. This impressive tome provides a detailed description of railway construction across the prairies and through the mountains of British Columbia and Alberta.

Cooper, Dene and Rob Alexander. *Exshaw: The Heart of the Valley*. Exshaw: The Exshaw Historical Society, 2005. Published as a centennial project, this 712-page book tells the story of the eastern end of the Canmore Corridor through family biographies and historical essays.

Hart, E.J. *The Place of Bows: Exploring the Heritage of the Banff-Bow Valley*. Banff: EJH Literary Enterprises, 1999. *The Place of Bows* and its companion volume, *Battle for Banff* (2003), are among the most comprehensive books on the history of Banff and the entire Bow Valley.

Further Reading

Keyser, James D. and Michael A. Klassen. *Plains Indian Rock Art*. Seattle: University of Washington Press, 2001. The fascinating stories of the Aboriginal people of western Canada are etched and painted onto rock walls, but few books explain the meaning of these enigmatic symbols. The authors of *Plains Indian Rock Art* include pictograph and petroglyph locations throughout the prairie provinces and neighbouring U.S. states.

Riva, Walter J. *Survival in Paradise: A Century of Coal Mining in the Bow Valley*. Canmore: Canmore Museum and Geoscience Centre, 2008. This book provides a complete history of coal mining in the Bow Valley, including the story of abandoned towns such as Georgetown, Anthracite, and Bankhead.

Snow, Chief John. *These Mountains are our Sacred Places: The Story of the Stoney People*. Calgary: Fifth House Publishers, 2005. *These Mountains are our Sacred Places*, authored by a prominent member of the Stoney-Nakoda, shares the history and culture of the Stoney people.

Spry, Irene M. *The Palliser Expedition: The Dramatic Story of Western Canadian Exploration 1857-1860*. Calgary: Fifth House, 1963. Spry's book is one of the first to tell the story of the 1857–1860 Palliser Expedition. The scientists involved in this expedition were the first to study western Canada and the Bow Valley region.

Yorath, Chris. *How Old is that Mountain? A Visitor's Guide to the Geology of Banff and Yoho National Parks*. Madeira Park: Harbour Publishing, 2006. Although Yorath's guide focuses more specifically on Banff and Yoho National Parks, this readable reference book unravels the complex nature of the Canadian Rockies.

Index

Alberta 14, 16, 20, 77, 100, 109, 119, 120, 121, 124, 129, 137, 148
Alberta census 83
Alberta Department of Mines and Minerals 130
Alberta Historical Resources Foundation 156, 157
Alberta Junior Hockey League 135
Alberta Municipal Government Act 168
Alberta Sports Hall of Fame 135
Alberta World Cup 164
Allan, Mount 158
Alpine Club of Canada 136, 163
Alpine Resort Haven 170
American Fur Company 26
Andrews, Paula 150, 164
Anthracite 46-47, 64, 71, 78, 79, 81, 90, 91, 93, 109, 116
Appleby, Edna 4, 100
Arrowheads 13
artsPeak 171
Ashk Development Corporation 154
Assiniboia 154
Assiniboine 31
Assiniboine, Mount 65, 136
Athabasca River 20
Athletes' Village 161, 164

Band Hall 83, 109
Banff 18, 32, 46, 79, 112, 114, 141, 153, 165
Banff National Park 8, 11, 12, 62, 103, 112, 117, 148, 150, 151, 161, 167
Banff Springs Golf Course 15
Bankhead 78-79, 85, 109, 114
Bears 29, 166
Bearspaw 16, 20, 21
Beaverfoot River 34
Benchlands Trail 161
Beringia 12
Berton, Pierre 87
Besant 12, 13
BHB Canmore Resorts 170
Biathlon Junior World Championships 164
Bighorn sheep 8, 11, 12, 16
Big head 51
Birney, Hester M. 84
Bison 8, 9, 10-11, 12, 16
Bison Historical Services 13
Black Diamond Property 70
Black Friday 145, 148
Black, Robert 150
Blackburn, Dan 134
Blackfoot 14, 15, 16, 18, 20, 26, 30, 31
Blackfoot Crossing 20

Index

Blakiston, Thomas 33
Blaney, Ambrose 115
Blood 15, 26
Bone, P. Turner 54
Bourgeau, Eugene 33, 34, 160
Bow-Canmore Area Market Demand Study 165
Bow Corridor Ecosystem Advisory Group 167
Bow Lake 34
Bow River 2, 12, 13, 15, 18, 20, 25, 26, 29, 34, 36, 43, 45, 62, 70, 74, 75, 77, 80, 81, 82, 83, 96, 97, 101, 105, 107, 110, 116, 117, 125, 126, 143
Bow River Gap 47
Bow Valley Eagles 135
Bow Valley Provincial Park 9
Bow Valley Trail 93, 118
Boxcar 54, 59
Boychuk, Johnny 162
Bragg Creek 160
Bray, Floyd 150
Brazeau 101
Bridge 80
Brinkerhoff 77
Briquette plant 110, 119, 128, 129, 138, 141
British Columbia 2, 19, 32, 36, 37, 42, 50, 74, 120, 129, 134, 148
British Empire 84
British Royal Navy 74
Broderick, Gid 100
Broderick, Neil 128
Brownlee, John Edward 117
Buffalo (see *Bison*)
Buffalo Nations Cultural Society 17
Buffalo Nations Luxton Museum 17
Byrne, Pat 150

C.T. Sing & Co 87, 125

Calgary 2, 13, 20, 31, 48, 50, 51, 70, 75, 90, 91, 100, 116, 120, 131, 154, 158, 160, 164
Calgary Herald, The 121, 143, 149, 152
Calgary Regional Planning Commission 154
Calgary Power 105
Campbell, Darcy 134
Camrose 101
Canada Cement Lafarge 148
Canada Day Parade 127
Canada Northwest Land Company 92
Canadian Alpine Centre 163
Canadian Anthracite Coal Co. 47, 71, 74, 77, 78, 79, 81, 82-83, 90, 93, 96, 97, 99, 100, 116, 117, 126, 135
Canadian Armed Forces 128
Canadian North-West Coal and Lumber Syndicate 77, 82
Canadian Pacific Railway 2, 8, 37, 39, 42, 44, 46, 50, 51, 54, 55, 59, 62, 64, 65, 70, 71, 74, 75, 78, 79, 80, 81, 85, 92, 93, 96, 101, 110, 113, 119, 126, 128, 130, 131, 135, 136, 137, 141, 160
Canadian Pacific Survey 37
Canadian Rockies 8, 11, 12, 42, 47, 62, 65, 136, 153, 162, 163
Canmore Canadians 134
Canmore Centennial Museum Society 3
Canmore Civic Centre 153, 171, 174
Canmore Coal Company 62, 97, 99, 103, 107, 108, 109, 117, 119, 124, 126, 136
Canmore Creek (see *Whiteman's Creek*)

Canmore Eagles 134, 135
Canmore Folk Music Festival 152, 171
Canmore Golf & Curling Club 9
Canmore Highland Games 171
Canmore Hospital 162
Canmore Hotel 4, 82, 85, 102, 107, 114, 130, 148, 171
Canmore Mines Ltd. 105, 126-127, 129, 130, 131, 137, 141, 143, 148, 149, 151
Canmore Museum and Geoscience Centre 4, 9, 152, 153, 171
Canmore Navigation and Coal Company 125
Canmore Nordic Centre 125, 142, 159, 161, 162, 164, 171
Canmore Recreation Centre 135, 153, 161
Canyon Dam 105
Caragata, Warren 106
Carbol, Leo 134
Carey, Charles 81, 91
Carey Creek 91
Carey Seam 110
Caribou 12
Carnegie, James 35
Carrot Creek Pass 25
Cascade Coal Basin 64, 67, 70, 74, 88, 130
Cascade Coal Company 46, 47, 64, 70
Cascade Coal District 67
Cascade Mountain 28, 34, 64, 70, 79
Cascade River 46, 64
Casey, Ron 150
Cashel, Ernest 46
Castle Mountain 37, 38, 103
Cemetery 92
Census 83, 84

Centennial Museum Society of Canmore 152, 153
Centennial Park 152
Centenary celebrations 152
Chakowski, Andy 134
Chicago Blackhawks 134
Chinaman's Peak 156
Chinese 48, 85, 86-88, 156
Chiniki 16, 20, 21
Chong, Lee 85
Chow, Alfred 156
Christianity 31, 32
Clarke, C.H. 104
Clarke, S.J. 113, 114
Clovis 12
Coal 62, 63, 64, 65, 66, 67, 69-93, 96-131, 134, 137, 138, 141, 152, 153, 172, 173
Coal Branch 101
Cochrane 75
Cochrane Mine 77, 82, 125
Cochrane, Sir Thomas B. 77
Coffee, Bill 58
Columbia Plateau Tradition 14, 19
Columbia River 42
Columbia Valley 14, 15, 25, 37
Commuter train 155
Compton, Charles 54
Conroy, James 58
Consolidated Coal Co. 79
Continental Divide 14, 15, 16, 25, 44
Cougar Creek development 161
Cougars 167
Coyotes 167
CPR (see *Canadian Pacific Railway*)
Craig, Glen 150
Craigellachie 50
Cree 25, 31
Cross Zee Ranch 162
Crowe, Thelma 135, 162

Index

Crowsnest Pass 93, 101, 126
Curling 111

Dailey, Pat 77
Dart point 15
Dawson City 65
Dawson, George Mercer 62-63
De Smet, Pierre Jean 28-29, 30, 62, 172
Dead Man's Flats 18, 93, 101, 105, 124, 142, 160, 168, 170
Deer 16, 166
Defeo, Joseph 89-90
Department of the Interior 92, 107, 111, 113, 114, 117, 149
Devil's Gap 25, 27
Devil's Head Creek 70
Dewis, Frederick 128
Diek, S.C. 84
Dillingham Corporation 143-144, 155, 165
District 18 120, 121
Dominion Parks Branch 79, 92, 111, 113, 114, 115, 116
Douglas, Howard 11, 115
Drumheller 101
Dry Lake 149
Dyck, Bert 150

E.L. Smith & Co 58
E.L. Little Co. 83, 99
Eagle Terrace 167
East End of Rundle 28
Eastern markets 121
Eau Claire and Bow River Lumber Company 75
Echo Valley 155
Ecklof, John 150
Edmonton 21, 31, 36, 101, 134, 173
Edmonton Oilers 155
Eighth Avenue 113, 142, 143, 150

Eighth Street 113, 116
Eleanor Luxton Historical Foundation 11
Electricity 105, 109, 110
Eleventh Street 117
Elk 16, 166
Elk Island National Park 11
Elk Run Boulevard 18
Elk Run development 161
Elks Band 83
Engine Bridge 80, 81, 113
Engine No. 4 129
England 32
Entwistle 101
Erasmus, Peter 16
Erickson, John 128
Exshaw 9, 12, 105, 112, 141, 148
Exshaw cement plant 105, 141

Ferry 82
Finn Hall 110, 111
Fire brigade 117, 173
Fleming, Sir Sandford 37, 38-39, 44
Flooding 46, 142-143
Foothills 14, 15, 16, 65
Fort Benton 44
Fort Edmonton 21, 26, 31, 34
Fournier, Lionel 162
Fur trade 20

Gabriel, Baptiste 36
Galt Mines 77, 78, 80
Gap, the 47, 48, 50
Gas industry 119
Geological Survey of Canada 62, 63, 74
Georgetown 124, 125
Glenbow Museum 59
Goat, The 129, 131, 138, 151
Golf course 150, 154, 155, 165, 169, 170, 171

179

Government of Canada 67
Grainger, Albert 62
Grainger Collieries 62, 119
Grainger Seam 119
Grand Trunk Pacific Railway 44
Grassi Lakes 19, 136
Grassi, Lawrence 136, 162
Great Depression 109, 119, 126, 135
Great Plains 14, 32
Grotto Canyon 19
Grotto Mountain 30, 34

H.W. McNeill Co. 79, 82, 83, 90, 93, 97, 99, 107
H.W. McNeill Co.'s Brass Band 83, 84
Ha Ling 156-157, 171
Ha Ling Peak 62, 156-157
Hamilton, Andrew 77
Hansen, J.P. 59
Harkin, J.B. 113, 114
Harmon, Byron 163
Harriott, James Edward 25, 26
Hart, E.J. (Ted) 30, 126
Harvie Heights 9, 152, 168
Hayes, Edmund 127, 128, 137
Hayes, Philip 137
Healy, Joe 43
Heart Creek 9, 10
Heart Mountain 34
Hector, James 16, 31, 33, 34, 35
Hector Lake 13
Hellis, Joseph 128
Henderson, Jessie Margaret 88
Heritage Park 131, 151
High school 150
Highway 1A 155, 162, 170
Hillcrest mine disaster 88
Hockey 134-135
Holt City 49, 50

Homesteads 165
Horseshoe 92, 111
Horseshoe Dam 105
Hospital 128, 148
Hospital Hill 125, 128
Hot springs 62
Howse Pass 11, 39
Hudson Bay 32
Hudson's Bay Company 21, 25, 26, 27, 31, 32, 36, 37
Hughes, Captain 70
Hydroelectric power 105

Ice rink 134
Ice skating (see *Skating*)
Imperial Order Daughters of the Empire 124
Improvement District No. 8 150
Incorporation 149-150, 173
Indian Flats 18, 34
Industrial park 150
Inflation 106
Influenza 106-107
Interior Salish 14, 19
Internment camps 103
Italians 90

Jackson, Percy 134
Japanese markets 138, 141, 143, 144
Jasper, town of 38, 44
Jasper National Park 20
Jerwa brothers 134
Joseph Chenier and Co. 59
Johnson Lake 70

Kainnai 15
Kaleta, Alex 134, 135
Kamloops 81
Kan-Can Resorts 170
Kananaskis 8, 34, 43, 45, 64, 75, 105, 141

Index

Kananaskis Country 8, 148, 151, 158, 165, 168, 173
Kananaskis Guest Ranch 170
Kananaskis Pass 34
Kananaskis River 43, 64
Kananaskis Valley 45, 75
Kay, Charles 11
Kernick, Frank 167, 169
KGM Developments 155
Kicking Horse Pass 2, 37, 39, 42, 43, 44, 45, 50
Kicking Horse River 34
Klotz, Pat 150
Kootenay 14, 15, 16, 19, 28
Kootenay Plains 11
Kootenay Valley 34

Lac des Arcs 9, 10, 34, 152
Lady Macdonald, Mount 55
Lafarge 148
Laggan 50
Lake Louise 49, 50, 51
Lake Minnewanka 8, 10, 12, 25, 78
Lake O'Hara 136
Lamphouse 4, 74, 149
Lamphouse Rise 165
Larch development 153, 161
Larch Avenue 143
Leduc 134, 135
Lethbridge 77, 101
Lewis, Evan 128
Loder Peak 24
Logging 75, 83
Lougheed, Mount 18, 34, 105, 160, 165
Lougheed, Peter 160
Lougheed, Sir James Alexander 160
Lusk, Thomas and Henrie 84
Luxton, Norman 11
Lynch, Stewart 100

Macdonald, John A. 2, 37
Mackenzie, Alexander 37
MacKinnon, H.G. 113
MacLaren, Alec 128
MacNulty Brothers General Store 58
Macoun, John 38
Mah Poy, Roger 156
Main Street 113, 150
Mammoth 8, 12
Manitoba 11, 120
Marra's Grocery 87, 125, 143
Marret, Francois 101
Marret, Jean 101
Marsh Mine 62, 64, 70
Maskepetoon 31
McCabe, Frank 62, 71
McCardell, Tom and William 62, 71, 77
McDougall family 43, 172
McGillivray, Duncan 25
McLean, George (see *Walking Buffalo*)
McLean, John 17
McLeod, John 128
McNeill, Hobart W. 5, 78, 79, 80, 81, 85, 86, 87, 91, 93
McNeill House 3, 96
McNeill, Walter 96, 97, 99, 108
McNeill, Wilbur 96
McTavish, John 51
MD of Bighorn 168, 170
Medicine Hat 81
Melchin, Richard 155
Memorial Hall 108, 109, 111
Metcalfe, Charles 26
Methodist Mission 43
Metis 25, 26
Michaluk, Art 134
Millen, William E. 150
Miltins, Dr. Alfred 149, 150

Miners Day 171
Miners' Relief Fund 129
Mineside 82, 83, 92, 109, 111, 115, 117, 125, 126, 134, 142, 143
Mining 2, 3, 69-93, 96-131, 134-145, 152, 153, 154, 173
Mining accidents 88-89
Model School 113
Montana 44
Morley 14, 18, 21, 26, 43, 172
Morris, James J. 107, 169
Morrow, M.B. 103, 104, 108
Motels and hotels 151, 152, 154, 155, 165
Mountain House 58, 59
Movie theatre 109
Mrokwia, Victor 145
Museum 153
Musgrove Slope 129

Nakiska 158, 164
Nakoda 15
National Resources Mobilization Act 128
Natural gas 134
Natural Resources Conservation Board 167, 168, 169
Nature Conservancy of Canada 167
Neale, James B. 97, 99, 100, 126
Ninth Avenue 113, 117
No. 1 Mine 71, 72-73, 74, 77, 80, 81, 85, 88, 93, 107, 110, 111, 115, 155, 173
No. 2 Mine 4, 96, 110, 144, 173
No. 3 Mine 119, 130, 142
No. 4 Mine 127, 129
No. 4B Mine 144
No. 5 Mine 130
Noble and Holy Order of the Knights of Labor 120
Non-permanent residents 170

North Kananaskis Pass 34, 36, 44
North West Company 21, 25, 26
North West Mounted Police 3, 46, 75, 90, 91, 102, 104, 172
North-West Territories 21, 32, 37, 102
Northern Pacific Railroad 42
Nova Scotia 65, 149
NWMP (see *North West Mounted Police*)
NWMP Barracks 4, 82, 91, 92, 171

Old Bow Fort (see *Peigan Post*)
Old Fort Creek 26
Olympic torch 162, 173
Olympics (see *Winter Olympic Games*)
One Big Union 121
Ontario 121, 124
OPEC 144
Opera House 83, 109, 126, 151
Oregon 25, 27
Oregon Improvement Co. 78
Oskaloosa Hotel 82, 101, 105, 109
Overlanders 36

Pacific States Steel 138
Padmore 43, 45, 50
Paleo-Indians 2, 12, 172
Palliser Expedition 32-34, 37, 43, 172
Palliser, John 33
Palliser Trail 92
Pan, Lee 113
Parks Act 117
Parks Branch (see *Dominion Parks Branch*)
Parks Canada 11, 12, 25, 151
Patrician Land Corp. 155, 158
Peaks of Grassi 165
Pearce, William 107

Index

Peechee, Mount 25
Peigan 15, 20
Peigan Post 25, 26, 35, 43, 45, 172
Pelican Lake Phase 10
Pembina 134, 137
Peters, F.H. 107
Peyto, Bill 163
Pictographs 19
Pigeon Mountain 34, 170
Piikini 15
Pine Tree Players 152
Pipestone Valley 34
Plains 15, 16, 28, 32
Pocklington, Peter 155
Policeman's Creek 91
Pond, Peter 21
Postmaster 59
Prehistoric life 9
Princess Margaret Mountain 25
Prisoners of war 103-104
Prohibition 102
Prospect 110
Public Works Department 85, 86

Quebec 121, 124
Quarry Lake 142, 157

Railway 2, 32, 37, 41-51, 62, 64, 66, 70, 75, 83, 85, 93, 126, 137, 160, 172
Railway Avenue 113
Railway station 51, 79, 172
Ralph Connor Memorial United Church 4, 82
Rat's Nest Cave 19
Red Deer River Valley 30
Red River carts 25
Redwater 134
Reid, Alexander P. 36
Reinikka, Ollie 134
Rhodda, H.A. 102

Riva, John 102
Riva, Walter 89, 141
Riverside Mine 144
Rocky Mountain Elk Foundation 167
Rocky Mountain House 21, 30
Rocky Mountains 30, 35, 37, 38, 63, 64, 65, 71
Rocky Mountains Park 11, 112, 117, 149, 173
Rodda, Alfonso 85
Rodda, Mary 85, 102
Rogers, A.B. 42-44, 45
Rogers, Albert 43, 45
Roundhouse 54, 55, 59
Royal Alberta Museum 35
Royal Commission 108, 129
Royal Geographic Society of London 32
Royal School of Mines 65
Rundle Crescent 92, 111, 125
Rundle Drive 83
Rundle Memorial United Church 31
Rundle, Mount 28, 31, 32
Rundle Mountain Trading Co. 83, 98, 99, 109, 111, 124
Rundle, Robert 30-32, 172
Rundle Rock 148
Rundleview development 155
Rupert's Land 32, 37

Sacred Heart Catholic Church 114
San Francisco 77
Saskatchewan 120, 129
Schaffer, Mary 163
Schoolhouse 51
Second Street 143
Section Avenue 55, 59
Sedlock, Joe 62
Seebe 167

Selkirk Mountains 42
Selwyn, Dr. Alfred R.C. 74
Seniors' lodge 150
Seventh Avenue 142
Seventh Street 114, 117
Sewage system 116
Shareholders' Cabin 116
Shuswap 15, 16
Sibbald Flats 12
Sibbald, Howard 114
Sidewalks 113
Siding 27 50, 54, 55, 62, 172
Siding 29 2
Siksika 15, 20
Silvertip 167, 169, 173
Sinclair, James 25, 26, 27, 33, 172
Skating 111, 134-135
Ski resort 155
Smith, Sir Donald 11, 51
Snow, John 161
South Canmore 143
Southesk, Earl of 35-36, 37, 39, 172
Sparrowhawk, Mount 158, 159
Sparwood 148
Spence, Major 103
Sputnik 139, 141
Spray Lake 154
Spray Lakes Sawmills 75
Spray River 15
Spray Valley 28, 43, 54, 55, 75, 93, 105, 158
Spring Creek Mountain Village 169
St. Louis Flyers 134
St. Michael's Anglican Church 4, 82, 117
Steel industry 138
Stewart, Archibald 91, 97, 100, 107, 115, 116, 127
Stewart brothers 70, 71
Stewart Creek Golf Course 149
Stewart Seam 129

Stone Creek Resorts 169
Stoney 15, 18, 20, 21, 31, 32, 162, 172
Stoney-Nakoda 12, 13, 16, 17, 19, 21
Stoney-Nakoda reserve 12, 13
Stoney Nakoda Resort 21
Strikes 79, 129
Strip Mine 141
Sullivan, John W. 33
Summit City 44

Teepee Town 155
Temple, Mount 65
TGS Properties 165
Thachuk, Nik 113, 114
Thompson, David 11, 24, 25, 28, 172
Thompson, S.A. 128
Thorne, Samuel Brinkerhoff 97, 99, 100, 126
Three Sisters, The 2, 5, 28, 118
Three Sisters Dam 105
Three Sisters Drive 63, 83, 125, 136
Three Sisters Mountain Village 9, 119, 155, 165, 167, 168, 169
Three Sisters Parkway 141
Three Sisters Royal Canadian Legion 109
Thunderstone Quarries 148
Tipis 18
Tipple 74, 76, 77, 82, 138, 140
Tofield 101
Toronto Bridge Co. 80
Tourism 126, 154, 165
Town hall 150
Townside 82, 108, 111, 113, 114, 115, 126
Toyo Menka 138, 140
Trail system 80, 161

Index

Trans-Canada Highway 8, 13, 21, 47, 141, 161, 167, 170
TransAlta 105
Treaty 7 20, 21
T'suu Tina 15, 20
Twin Lakes 136
Typhoid fever 107
Tyrrell, Joesph 65

Underwood McLellan and Associates Ltd. 154
Union Hall 4, 106, 120, 121, 130, 144
Union Pacific Railroad 37
Unions 120-121, 124
United Mine Workers of America 120
United States 37, 42, 121
University of Calgary 162
U.S. Bureau of Equipment 74

Van Horne, William Cornelius 54, 70, 78, 79, 80, 81, 169
Vancouver 74
Vavasour, Mervin 27, 28, 29
Verdiso, John 101
Vermilion Lakes 8, 10, 12
Vermilion Pass 34, 37
Vick, S.C. 58
Village Townhouses 165

Walker, Colonel James 75
Walker strip mine 144
Walking Buffalo 17
Warre, Henry James 26-28, 29, 172
Waverly Hotel 82
Wesley 16, 20, 21
Western Federation of Miners 120
Weyerhaeuser, Frederick E. 97, 99
Wheatley, Frank 109
Wheeler, Arthur 163

White, Cliff 11
White Man Pass 28, 29
Whiteman's Creek 62, 71, 74, 86, 107, 110, 172
Whiteman's Gap 25, 26, 27, 28, 29, 34, 43, 105, 172
Whyte Museum of the Canadian Rockies 163
Whyte, William 80
Wildlife corridors 166-167
Williamson, Annie 134
Wilson Mine 141
Wilson, Tom 163
Wilson, William 141
Wind Mountain 105, 160
Wind Ridge 18, 62, 70, 105, 119
Windtower 18, 160
Wind Valley 18, 105, 119, 141, 142, 155, 165, 168
Windy Mountain 34
Winter Olympic Games 158-165, 166, 173
Witham, Norman 3
Wolves 8, 167
Workmens Compensation Board 108
World War I 100, 101, 105, 106, 109, 119, 121, 172
World War II 126, 128, 130, 134, 138, 152, 172
Worthington, Doctor 107

Yamnuska, Mount 9
Yanos, Joe 128
Yellow Head Pass (also *Yellowhead Pass*) 38, 39, 42, 44
Yop, Pearl 156
Young, Allan 128
Young, Robert M. 99
Yukon Territory 65

Photo Credits

Summerthought Publishing would like to thank the following individuals, museums, and archives for permission to reproduce their work.

Alexander, Rob: p. 9, p. 10, p. 13, p. 15

Canmore Museum and Geoscience Centre: p. 3, p. 23, p. 53, p. 58, p. 69, p. 76, p. 83, p. 86, p. 87, p. 89, p. 91, p. 95, p. 96, p. 97, p. 98, p. 106, p. 108, p. 115, p. 120, p. 122-123, p. 125, p. 131, p. 133, p. 134, p. 139, p. 140, p. 150

Glenbow Museum: front cover (na-3740-5; William Notman), p. 5 (na-937-2; S.J. Thompson), p. 17 (na-714-21; Dan McCowan), p. 29 (na-568-1), p. 31 (na-642-1), p. 33 (na-588-1), p. 35 (na-1355-1; T.R. Williams), p. 38 (na-3840-5), p. 43 (na-1949-1), p. 44 (na-1679-12; Edgar Spurgeon), p. 48-49 (na-1432-17; Oliver Buell), p. 53 (na-4967-29; Oliver Buell), p. 56-57 (na-1909-5), p. 59 (na-3271-4), p. 66-67 (na-3740-5; William Notman), p. 72-73 (na-4074-5; Daisy Carroll), p. 75 (na-3535-211; S.A. Smyth), p. 111 (na-3346-1; Trueman), p. 135 (na-2536-10), p. 142 (na-3342-3), p. 172 (na-1355-1; T.R. Williams), p. 173 upper (na-1909-5), back cover (na-937-2; S.J. Thompson)

Hempstead, Andrew: p. 1, p. 4, p. 63, p. 81, p. 85, p. 93, p. 137, p. 147, p. 149, p. 153, p. 157, p. 158-159, p. 160, p. 166, p. 169, p. 173 lower

Library and Archives Canada: p. 27 (C-001618; Henry Warre),

Mahaska Memories Project: p. 80

Whyte Museum of the Canadian Rockies: p. 7 (v527-ng-124; Mary Schaffer), p. 41 (v10-na66-680), p. 47 (v653-ng-26), p. 61 (v701-lc-223), p. 78 (na66-459), p. 84 (v532-na66-1888), p. 112 (na33-797), p. (v469-993; George Noble), p. 118 (v469-2691; George Noble), p. 127 (na66-134; Bert Prendergast), p. 163 (na66-186)

Acknowledgments

A book of this nature relies on the work and support of others. The writings of Edna Appleby, Walter J. Riva and E.J. (Ted) Hart were invaluable resources for *The History of Canmore*. I am also indebted to proofreaders Ian A. L. Getty, Emerson Sanford, Gerry Stephenson, and Cathy Jones, all of whom helped create a better book by pointing out errors and misconceptions in early drafts. I would also like to thank Julie E. Hansen, librarian at the Wilcox Library at the William Penn University in Oskaloosa, Iowa, for providing permission to use the portrait of H.W. McNeill. Until now, McNeill had been a prominent, but faceless figure in Canmore's past. The same could be said for information provided by Rev. Professor Elijah J. Bremer, of the History/Humanities Department at Pennsylvania Highlands Community College, which allowed me to learn more about S.B. Thorne and James B. Neale of the Canmore Coal Company. Dr. Trevor Peck, a plains archaeologist with Historic Resources Management—Archaeological Survey provided an extensive and useful list of resources with all of the known published references and a bibliography pertaining to Canmore and its earliest human history. I am grateful to the staff of the Canmore Museum & Geoscience Centre—including Edward van Vliet, Mary-Beth Laviolette, Debbie Carrico and Eva Tkaczuk—who provided support, advice, and access to the archives and the resources it contains. Summerthought publisher Andrew Hempstead and editor Rachel Small did great service organizing the manuscript, providing polish, and asking questions that sent me back to my notes and sources to provide clarity.

Finally, I would like to thank my wife, Cathy, for giving me the space and support I needed to write this book.

About the Author

Rob Alexander grew up in Canmore, steeped in the history of the Canadian West and the sights and sounds of a coal mining town. With an affinity for ruins and abandoned sites, he gravitated towards story and sense-of-place leading him to study writing and photography. He is a reporter for the *Rocky Mountain Outlook* newspaper, a freelance writer and co-author of *Exshaw: Heart of the Valley* and *The Exshaw Cement Plant: Foundations for the Future*. He and his wife, Cathy, were married in the Canmore Miners' Union Hall in 2008 and their daughter, Alaina, was born in Canmore in 2009.